SIMPLE GIFTS

Your relationships as a spiritual path

Simple tools, maps, guides to reveal and heal the hidden conspiracy against knowing who you really are!

James F. Shea, BA, MA, CHT.

BALBOA
PRESS
A DIVISION OF HAY HOUSE

Balboa Press books may be ordered through booksellers or by contacting:

Balboa Press
A Division of Hay House
1663 Liberty Drive
Bloomington, IN 47403
www.balboapress.com
1 (877) 407-4847

Because of the dynamic nature of the Internet, any web addresses or links contained in this book may have changed since publication and may no longer be valid. The views expressed in this work are solely those of the author and do not necessarily reflect the views of the publisher, and the publisher hereby disclaims any responsibility for them.

The author of this book does not dispense medical advice or prescribe the use of any technique as a form of treatment for physical, emotional, or medical problems without the advice of a physician, either directly or indirectly. The intent of the author is only to offer information of a general nature to help you in your quest for emotional and spiritual well-being. In the event you use any of the information in this book for yourself, which is your constitutional right, the author and the publisher assume no responsibility for your actions.

Any people depicted in stock imagery provided by Thinkstock are models, and such images are being used for illustrative purposes only. Certain stock imagery © Thinkstock.

Print information available on the last page.

ISBN: 978-1-5043-4997-0 (sc)
ISBN: 978-1-5043-4999-4 (hc)
ISBN: 978-1-5043-4998-7 (e)

Library of Congress Control Number: 2016907639

Balboa Press rev. date: 09/22/2016

Contents

Preface

This is a simple book. It has to be, otherwise it might never get written. I have already attempted to write this book at least twice, only to get bogged down part of the way through the writing in the drudgery of unnecessarily complicated explanations, of needlessly complex material.

There is an inherent danger in endeavoring to bring simplicity to the many deeper and more challenging issues in life. The danger is in being viewed as overly simplistic and dismissed out of hand. I believe, however, the rewards of finding a true resolution far outweigh any of these potential challenges.

Does this book need to be written? Well, if it can help, even a little, in simplifying and resolving any of the deeper challenges everyone faces at this time, then I say yes it is worth it. Actually, it is not my purpose to provide actual solutions to these challenges. Rather, I wish to offer a set of guidelines, heuristic processes, helpful charts and maps for arriving at these solutions yourself.

Simply put, anything which is capable of reducing and/or eliminating pain and suffering, or the amount of time it takes to realize the deeper truths of your life, is truly a gift. This is my simple gift to you.

So it is with this intention and an abundance of good will that I offer these approaches for you to check out for yourself. If they work for you, even a little, it has been worthwhile. If not, I thank you for your kind consideration and wish you well in your further search.

Introduction

In writing this little book, I felt it important to initially share some of the guiding influences to its creation. These "guides" or "influences" are in the form of critical autobiographical information. To this end, I have included an extended portion of background in this Introduction.

Since these influences often seem to come from sources that cannot be documented, I have little option but to share as much as I can about the context of their arrival in my life. I trust that the reader will grant me this. Having come from a logical background that is well grounded in scientific documentation, I can see the challenges that this may represent for some. I honor your choice.

Nothing happens by chance. All of the surrounding factors of any given event, while material to that event, may never be fully known. To the best of my memory and knowledge, I have captured the basic elements surrounding some of the key events leading up to the writing of this book. My goal has been to keep it as simple, accessible and as free of extraneous material as possible.

The most important key to keep in mind is that this is not a book of solutions. It is a book of heuristic* ideas, devices and guidelines to assist those who are wishing to free themselves from limitations, illusions, traps, and heal the ego conspiracy against their Greatness. These have worked for me, and I am grateful for the guidance I have received, regardless of where it came from. I have been blessed to have had this guidance, and I am deeply honored to share these simple gifts with you.

*Definition of "Heuristic"

- **Encouraging discovery of solutions: relating to or using a method of teaching that encourages learners to discover solutions for themselves.**
- **May involve trial and error: using or arrived at by a process of trial and error rather than set rules.**
- **Able to change: can describe a computer software program that modifies itself in response to the varying conditions it encounters.**
- **Experience-based exploratory techniques for problem solving, learning, and discovery.**
- **A way to grow that does not involve rigid dogmatic, black and white requirements.**

These gifts arrive in the form of heuristics and are intended to support and liberate your natural gifts and guide your movement through the ego's conspiracy toward the truth of your Higher Being – your Greatness.

As you will come to see, it all begins with moments of awareness and grows from there. The heuristics are your ticket to these moments. I encourage you to check out and explore each and everything you find along the way.

Try it on, see if it's a fit. We wouldn't buy a new piece of clothing without trying it on first, so why is it not at least equally important with our mind and its contents?

The early chapters are essentially establishing a basis that can permit an open inquiry and that can offer a foundation and framework on which to build. Treat every chapter and its contents as an invitation to an exercise in true heuristic exploration. I have debated with myself whether to leave the autobiographical information in the book, or to take it out. I have chosen to leave it in, as it conveys an extra element of depth that is not only relevant and material to the development of this book but also shares a personal reflection of the author that is often missing in an endeavor of this sort. Enjoy my following story.

......

There was something about making people laugh that just delighted me. I always wanted to play the clown, the comedian. I still do. I also wanted to set up a humor therapy institute to take advantage of the healing energy that is associated with laughter. Clearly, I did not make it on either count. I believe I have been guided throughout my life in quite a different direction.

While my high school years were somewhat bleak, University felt like coming home. The friends and the people I met there were wonderful in a way I cannot fully describe. We were a community of souls that inspired and uplifted each other. In this environment I flourished and managed to complete my undergraduate degree in Honors Psychology and English in three years.

My Masters in Psychology was a much more competitive affair, and while I was the first to graduate, I did not enjoy the feelings of separation engendered by the competition. In addition, the heavy focus on behaviorism seemed void of meaning and soul. My thesis was on levels of curiosity in elementary school children as a factor in learning. It was as close as I could get to real life and away from black box psychology.

I remember debating whether I should continue on to my PhD. I discussed this matter with my mentor, a tenured professor, and his response was, "You have to...it's your union card...your security card." I explained that it felt like a form of prostitution to do it that way...he smiled and left. I enrolled in my PhD program at the University of London, England and began to explore my academic opportunities. I had corresponded with my thesis supervisor prior to deciding on a PhD location, and there was agreement that I would continue my MA research as the basis for my doctorate in London.

However, when I arrived and met with my supervisor, he advised me that if I planned to go the "supported" route, I would carry out my research on some aspect of his theory, which meant carrying out my thesis on "conditioned eye blink." My other alternative was to go ahead on my own without support, dealing with the problems of pursuing my research without all of the necessary resources I would need in order to finish.

My supervisor told me to take some time off, go on a little holiday and relax before making my decision. Instead, I wandered the halls and spent a lot of time in the Library where I began to explore the lives of the Eastern Mystics, which I found incredibly interesting. This, I thought, was not helping my situation at all. Each day, as I walked down the hall toward the library, I would walk by a copy of Edvard Munch's "The Scream." I felt as if it was my portrait.

One day, I was walking down in Soho when I heard this incredible laughter. It sounded great to my ears but as I turned around I saw what I thought was a crazy hobo coming to attack me in a fit of mania. As he got closer there was something familiar amidst all the hair on his face. It was one of my best friends from undergraduate school. What a glorious sight! As we hugged, he told me he had just arrived, which was clear from the backpack on his back. We both recognized the unlikely odds of meeting "by chance" in a city with a population of over 10,000,000 people at that time.

This was, of course, not by chance. He joined me, and daily we would read from Leonard Cohen, Richard Brautigan, and listen to music. Jimi Hendrix died that year at the Isle of Wight music festival from a drug overdose; Janis Joplin died shortly thereafter.

It grew harder and harder for me to continue in my program, even though I only had to complete my thesis. Later, I would write in an article for Common Ground Magazine:

> "It has been many years since that day in the library at the University of London in England. I was working on my PhD and all I had left was to write my thesis in order to graduate. I had research and scholarship money that placed me on an income level higher than my professors were earning and lived in what was considered 'luxury accommodations.' I had two potential university level teaching positions waiting and a future that perfectly matched the goals that I had set for myself...and I was dying from the inside out.

> I didn't know this at the time, only that I was deeply uninspired and unhappy. It was that day, as I sat in the library feeling so separate, that things began to change. I had just come across a picture in a book I was browsing through of a naked man with outstretched arms entitled,

'I accept....' Underneath it was written, 'Where the vision is absent a people perish.' I became overwhelmed with a mixture of deep terror, pain and a sadness bordering on despair. I headed for the washroom, locked myself in one of the stalls and began to sob helplessly, praying that no one would come in. It seemed like such a long time before I could regain some level of composure. Just as I was getting control of myself again, I happened to glance at the wall of the stall I was in. Written at just about eye level was the graffiti quote, 'Suicide is the severest form of self-criticism.' I was gone again, sobbing inconsolably.

What happened that day in the library was that I realized I was not doing what I had come to the planet to do. I had not at all accepted my purpose for being here and was slowly dying amidst my accomplishments and achievements. It was a kind of passive suicide. Who could have suspected? I was giving up on my highest vision, and in the process, the hopes and dreams of my heart. It was the deepest sadness I had ever experienced.'"

As I gradually emerged from this graveyard, so has my Vision and my desire to touch as many lives as I could. There are many of us who came to share their higher vision but it is a challenging thing to live. Many are as yet unwilling to take the risk. These gifts of vision are gifts of hope and empowerment, capable of bringing people back from the brink of death, back to life. Yet, to be real, our vision would require that we live it. It is a vision that asks that we be present and responsive right here, right now, lighting the way. It doesn't have to be perfect, but it does have to be present. Not one single person need go down in the darkness if all of us, who were called, would respond. It is a vision conceived by Angels, as a Grace for mankind and can be heard only by that part of us that is Angelic. It whispers to each of us: 'You are Complete the way you are. Your being here is a Grace for everyone. The time is Now to unveil the tenderness of your heart and give your presence to the world. This is your Gift of Greatness. This is your Vision of Hope. This is your Legacy of Love.

(Used with the permission of Common Ground Magazine Vancouver)

During my time in London, I had several experiences that served as "spiritual guiding" experiences for me. In one such experience I had a severe migraine and was resting on my bed, in a kind of twilight state when all of a sudden I experienced myself travelling through a tunnel upwards toward a bright light. I was intensely communicating that I wanted to come home. I wanted out.

Needless to say, I was refused, but I kept insisting. I remember I was communicating with these beings of light who were refusing me and who made it quite clear it was not my time. I still had more to do. The last thing I recall was feeling a momentum taking me back down the tunnel and these beings communicating something to me. But everything they were communicating, as I moved farther and farther away, was being converted to musical notes I could not understand.

During this time, I recall going to see a movie in London, *Getting Straight*, starring Elliott Gould and Candice Bergen. Leonard Maltin would comment decades later that while the film was essentially a "period piece," its central issue revolved around a graduate student needing to choose between the academic doubletalk and his own deeply held truth and values. The classic scene and pivotal moment comes as Gould's character, Harry, is defending his Master's thesis, and a question arises about F. Scott Fitzgerald's sexuality, (which Gould's character had apparently overlooked). Fumbling for an answer, he struggles to his feet and climbs up on the committee room table and in a fit of anger creates absolute havoc as he expounds on the decline of the limerick.

His professor asks, "Why Harry? Why throw it all away like that? What are you going to do now?" to which Harry replies, "Don't you understand? It's not what you do that counts, it's what [who] you are." Shortly after that, I made the decision to leave my program. It was tough, because I had invested so much of my life in academia, yet it wasn't my Truth to stay.

It was following this particular period that I recall having a series of dreams. One such dream involved being a "light being" and moving through fields of crystals with other light beings. We were searching for something within these fields, but I was unclear as to what it was we were actually searching for. We moved in kind of a floating and gliding motion, and it seemed to me we were looking for some kind of crystal. I was quite junior amongst these beings and not really sure why I was even there since this all seemed so important to them. The next thing I knew I was hovering over a location that had already been explored and wondering what in hell was going on. I had inadvertently found what "we" were looking for. I looked down at it. There was a dark opening, like a crack or lengthwise hole with a powerful energy flowing from it. I didn't know what to make of it.

The others instantly stopped and moved back toward me. There was a shocked and quizzical expression on their countenances. I suspect there was also one on mine as well. They gathered around and determined, in a surprised and puzzled way, that this was, in fact, what "we" were looking for.

"Why me?" I thought. "Why him?" they said. A discussion followed. I got that they not only saw me as too immature, but also lacking in any real experience. I had no idea what was going on, why I was with them on this quest, or what I had found.

One of them, a senior member, came over to me where I was still hovering above the crack. He said, "We have decided that since you have found this, you must go!" I had not the slightest idea what he was talking about and before I could find out, I found myself transported to what seemed to me to be a grave. I was about to be buried alive! I was filled with terror when the senior member appeared above me. I looked up and in addition to the abject fear that was there I was filled with a deep sense of sadness and betrayal.

He looked down at me and smiled compassionately. His gentle eyes seemed to remove all that I was feeling. I suddenly felt his Love, and then my excitement, and I knew at least for the time being I was okay. I briefly seemed even to know what was happening.

Then my fear returned, although not as bad as before, and I asked, "How will I ever get back? How will I find you?" "You will know when it is time to follow the light," he replied to me. I did not feel nearly as comforted by this. "What if I can't find it or miss it?" He smiled again, that tender loving smile. Then everything went blank. This was all I could remember of this dream.

Later, I had a similar dream where I was entering into a pyramid through an opening at the base of the pyramid. It was an initiation rite, as part of the process of becoming a High Priest. I needed to find my way through the pyramid in the pitch black darkness. I had to avoid falling into the areas that were open to a long, downward passage, or getting so caught up in my own fear to the point where I became paralyzed and could not move. There were many turns, like a labyrinth, and I had to find my way out. I have no memory beyond this point but recalling the dream brings up stress. I wondered if there was possibly something larger going on of which I was unaware. Why all these dreams? Am I ready? Ready for what?

To prepare myself, I went for training at Oscar Ichazo's Arica, a 40-day psycho-spiritual program. During this period, I had several "guiding experiences." Before the program even started, my first night I had a dream in the form of images which offered me direction and affirmed my choice to be there. I was in the experience of this dream through the whole night and awoke in the morning refreshed, inspired and with an image of Grace, a huge white screen bathed in light.

Arica, while pretty heady, was very focused on aligning the body, mind and spirit using Psycho-calisthenics, Eurhythmics, Meditation and Chanting. During a set of Kath generation postures, I had an out of body experience and a connection with a higher level of this particular experience. I was in a standing position, with legs slightly bent and arms in front slightly bent. We were expected to hold these positions for a 20-30 minute period without moving. For me, it was excruciatingly painful. I refused to give up, even though my body was aching and vibrating like a freshly plucked string. Sweat was pouring off of me, and then I hit this place where I felt I could not go on or I would go unconscious.

It was at this point that I found myself outside my body and standing quietly beside it. What was interesting was that I felt no pain, no vibration, no sweat. Instead, I felt very tranquil, calm, and comfortable, even though it was clear that my body was still experiencing the pain. The energy of the experience was clearly a training exercise, but I felt a high level of spiritual guidance in relation to this exercise and preparing myself for whatever lay ahead.

One other Arica experience involved chanting the mantra "Holy Love" for long periods as a group. I was barely underway, trying to tune my voice to that of the group when I lost consciousness. I only became aware of this after coming back. I don't exactly know what happened while I was away, but I felt an enormous amount of love radiating from my heart as the chanting ended. This carried over into my daily life.

As I looked at others, especially people on the street, I would make eye contact and it was like a "micro star flash" would pass between us. Almost always it would result in the most beautiful connection… no words, no contact (beyond the eye contact), just the sweet experience of the "Love Connection."

I was one "happy chappy" throughout the extended period of this experience of two weeks. I thought it would last forever, but it didn't. It was like being taken to the mountain top and experiencing this beautiful state and then being taken back to where I was before and left to now climb the mountain and get there on my own. I still do this chant in meditation.

I eventually took a teacher's training course in California with Yogi Bhajan to learn the energetic secrets of Kundalini Yoga and prepare my body for whatever level of energetic vibrations.

Yogi Ji, as we called him, put on a tantric yoga program which really had a powerful effect on all of us. It was, in fact, very challenging to manage this energy. It seemed like everything that was highest and lowest in us surfaced for healing. This was certainly what I had come for. I eventually became a qualified Kundalini yoga teacher and headed home to share these gifts.

Following a period of time to integrate, I decided to open an educational institute to teach Mind-Body exercises using the 3HO Kundalini Yoga, along with the Arica Psychocalisthenics. This felt like it was what I really needed to be doing. I would occasionally feel the "Love Connection," even with individuals that I think may have been on drugs. This Institute period was limited because it didn't take long before we reached pretty much all of those who were open to what we offered. It was just a bit out of sync with where the majority of people were…like opening a liquor store in the Bible Belt. I decided to move on.

I applied to the Synthesis Graduate School in San Francisco for another go at my PhD. It offered Advanced Counseling Training in Psychosynthesis, and once I began, my life seemed to open up considerably. I began to more fully offer myself in service to others. It was wonderful to share in the spiritual growth of others and to be a part of what seemed to me to be minor transformational miracles.

The experiences of being in service, in community, and there for others led me to create alternative living environments for the developmentally challenged and for individuals experiencing autism spectrum disorder. These were small integrated communities which did not stand out in the neighborhood. They were home to a maximum of four clients with a high staff to client ratio. We viewed them as an alternative to the group home system which typically housed eight or more people and which definitely stood out. In spite of the client behavioral issues we were challenged with, we lived together for almost two decades and it was one of the most meaningful experiences up to that point in my life.

During this period, there were a series of dreams I had each night over a period of several weeks. I came to call them "number 3" dreams because they all seemed to center around the number 3. It was quite an inspiration, as I would experience the dream and drink in the wisdom I was exposed to. It was absolutely wonderful until I would try to wake up enough to share it with my partner, only to discover that all memory of the dream had evaporated, and I was left unable to communicate anything about the dream, except the number 3 and a sense that everything was going to be just fine. What that referred to, I really don't know, but that was the outcome of each of the dreams. I felt that there was a relevance to these dreams to my life but had no idea specifically how.

During this period I felt drawn to breathwork/rebirthing, which is a simple form of restoring natural breathing using a circular breathing method. It is a very powerful method of healing using the breath to restore flow. During a ten week breath work session, as I reached a point of integration, I suddenly saw and felt the presence of an immense shining light. As I moved towards it, I began to feel a level of fear. I was being invited to ascend. I paused, the level of fear escalated. I only felt loss. I began to think about all the people I knew. My partner, my son, my family, my clients, and I felt I could not leave them. I communicated that it was not the right time, that I still had work to do.

It was bizarre, as I thought about it. Was this the light that had been referred to by the "senior member?" Would I miss the chance to rise? Was it attachment and I could not let go? I only knew the desire to stay and give my gifts to all those I loved was paramount. I had a memory of regret regarding past lives that I had not always given all that I could. I was sure I should stay, and as that thought expressed, the light was gone. Even as I drove home after the session, I felt gratitude that I had the honor and blessing of giving my simple little gifts in whatever form they took.

Then I discovered Psychology of Vision, Dr. Chuck Spezzano, a gifted workshop presenter, and as I watched him sharing his love, it gradually became clear to me exactly what I wanted to be doing, in one form or another, for the balance of my life. No one had ever had the effect on me that Chuck had. It was like recognizing someone I had known from before, but I couldn't quite understand what was going on. No one was doing what Chuck was doing. It was the first time I had seen anyone who so epitomized a "Vision of Love," that could actually heal people.

When I did the first of Chuck's workshops, I felt a deep pain in my heart which I knew was my heart opening. I wanted to learn all I could from him. He seemed to know things I had yet to realize. He was a personification of my deepest vision and this dramatically accelerated my growth. It inspired me to begin to share my presence and express my Love and through the workshop format to reach more people than I could ever have hoped for just seeing one person at a time.

I knew I had made the right decision and felt a deep sense of gratitude to my spiritual guides and their spiritual guidance... but now it was up to me. All the guidance, education and effort were not going to get me where I wished to be if I wasn't able to ground and apply it.

To say I felt challenged is a huge understatement. I would over prepare for my workshops and then have to back off, since I was being guided to surrender to the flow of the energy that was present in the group. I was still struggling with the whole idea of letting go and receiving the guidance that was necessary there in the moment. I had run into the same issue, initially, in my one to one guiding. It is not something you can think your way through. And yet, letting go of my ego in order to surrender to a higher guidance was very challenging. It felt like being on a trapeze and needing to let go and trust that you would be caught by the "other artist."

In counseling, one of the big differences between a good guide and a great guide is the quality of their surrender, their connection with the client. It means the difference between being fully present with the client and just operating out of a theoretical paradigm which may or may not have relevance for the client. I had to take that leap of faith, or it was all in vain.

What's more, working with a group and finding that point of surrender and the connection with the group that could facilitate letting go, was a much more challenging proposition than one-to-one, at least initially. It was as I struggled to release myself that I got my first early lessons in dealing with the ego. The first thing I noticed as I explored my predicament was that I seemed to be in a very powerful trance, and how trapped I felt in this place. I knew, from my one-to-one work that it had taken a lot to free myself from my fear and my inner script of how things should go in order to let all things be the way they actually were, in the moment, with my client.

I began to use a style of heuristic, an "as if true" exploration, that I had created in University to help with generating more alternatives in places where I felt stuck. In my mind, I would create an "as if" condition, or a "free state", where I was not at all stuck and where I was free to move in any direction that I chose. Then I could observe and see if this revealed anything that I was not already aware of, or even if I was actually stuck.

It wasn't long before it became clear that I was indeed trapped by the illusion of fear. This fear based condition, revealed by the heuristic exercise, reminded me of a situation I had seen, wherein a man had been placed in a circle and hypnotized to believe he could not get out of the circle even though nothing blocked him. Even though he struggled he was unable to release himself. I felt like I was that man, only I was encircled by a belief in fear instead of a circle, and I was under a spell of my own ego's creation.

I had been here before and managed to set myself free by using a heuristic approach to not only discover how I was holding myself back but also how to set myself free. What I discovered by letting myself believe and behave as if I was free was that in fact I was free, as long as I remained fully in the moment and gave my fullest attention to the client or group I was working with. If I became even the slightest bit "self-conscious", it was gone in an instant, and I was left filled with fear, awkwardness and incredible discomfort. It was like I was going to be exposed at any minute as an imposter, and that I really knew nothing at all of what I was talking about. I had dared to step out of my ego's circle. Now I was going to pay.

That was the bad news, the good news was that the minute I restored the "as if" condition and allowed myself to be fully present in the moment and focused on the client or group, I was beyond the realm of the ego again. In fact, I also discovered that the more deeply I could feel my love for whomever I was with, the more powerful was this "transpersonal" state, a state beyond the purely personal level.

Such was the journey that led me to this point in my life and an awareness of the challenge that now lay before me. It clearly had to do with the recognition of how limiting the experience of being trapped by the ego is, and yet how do you set yourself free when you have no idea you are trapped.

Now, before I get ahead of myself, and too far down the road of sharing these little gifts, I had best lay some basic groundwork and a simple device that can form a foundation for the exploring the content of the book.

Initially, we will explore the very practical gift of the "as if" heuristic. It really is the key to how much value this book will have for you, in moving through the content that follows and transforming old limiting attitudes and beliefs. I can't emphasize enough the importance of this one simple gift.

Thank you for coming this far with me. I wish you well on your unique journey. I hope we meet somewhere along the way. Bon Voyage.

James Shea, December, 2013

Chapter 1

If It Isn't Broken, Why Fix It?

**"In truth, there is nothing wrong...
anywhere, and all is exactly as it should
be in God's creation. And yet people are
suffering and dying painful deaths, while war,
sickness and poverty still cover an enormous
percentage of the planet. How do we resolve
this seemingly irresolvable paradox?"**

This book really has more to do with discovering your own
explanation of the above than reading anyone else's. Rather, we
offer a set of simple heuristic approaches to discovering your
own solutions and applying these for yourself.

I have come to discover that actual originality and true
creativity are hard to claim, but to the best of my knowledge
all that is presented is original. Perhaps, it may be best viewed
as a creative editing of a lifetime's exposure to the wisdom of
the world.

Books abound offering explanations for all of the more
profound and perplexing issues of life. These may even offer
useful insights and possibly reasonable explanations. The
question is – **Are they your insights?** If they aren't then they

will have little likelihood of having more than just a fleeting value in your life.

As Werner Erhard commented, "Understanding is the booby prize." If you only understand something and stop there as if that was it, you never really get to apply it in your life. This happens to be the single greatest challenge to people who are seeking solutions in their lives today. The proverbial coin has not yet dropped into their experience, only into their awareness. As a result, it does not get applied in their life.

For example, I remember in high school reading poems and having a sense of the structural design and general meaning of the poem. It was only when I got to university that I began to understand what the poem was about through the richness and texture of words, sounds, images, and rhymes. It was as if I had discovered new levels of meaning...the coin had just dropped. The poem took on personal meaning for me. I had made it my own through experiencing different levels of understanding.

How can heuristics help us to discover deeper meanings in our lives? Is this really a gift? How can this improve our lives?

Go back to the quotation at the beginning of this chapter and read it again. It is an interesting paradox that "Everything is exactly as it should be in God's creation, and yet people are suffering and dying painful deaths, while war, sickness and poverty still cover an enormous percentage of the planet."

So how do you explore this paradox from a heuristic viewpoint?

We must first be prepared to take a heuristic idea (just one at a time), and live it "as if true" for us, for at least a few weeks, (three to six weeks). Only then can we say with any real basis in actual application, what our true experience of this heuristic is and has been.

I encourage you to do just that, and to live your life with your heuristic "as if true" for the three to six week period. Longer is usually better than shorter, but at least you will have a sense of how to explore from a heuristic viewpoint.

While it is a simple approach the results can be quite profound. There is a heuristic exercise in the appendix if you would like a guideline on how to evaluate your experience.

Chapter 2

Discovering...Discovery

"Most people live their lives according to rules and dogma they have internalized from the culture, family, friends, religion, school system, etc. Is that a good way to live your life? Possibly for some it may be. However, as a strategy of living, it is limited, because it is not an approach that supports growth, creativity, and discovery. It does not permit the exploration, investigation, or experience of new ideas, or beliefs if they may run counter to the rules, dogma, culture or religion."

As a student I searched for a philosophy of life that was robust enough to withstand continual interrogation and questioning. I did not particularly enjoy having my most recent set of beliefs about life and how to live it shot down by a better, more compelling system of beliefs.

During the first week of my freshman year of university, I sat in the student lounge, listening to the discussions taking place among the senior students regarding some of the larger questions of life. I found it incredibly stimulating and profoundly intriguing to listen to everyone who shared an opinion about their own beliefs.

Some were in direct opposition to each other, but the spirit of discovery lifted each beyond the limitations of being right and propelled the group toward a higher truth. I was so excited I could not sleep that night.

Later in the year, I took a philosophy course, and was stuck at a particular place in my quest. At the end of class I went up to the professor to ask him about it. I said, "Excuse me Professor, I am being driven crazy by a question I can't seem to find an answer to." He paused briefly, as he was gathering up his notes, looked at me directly, and simply replied, "Good." Then he turned and walked out of the room. I was left to work it out for myself rather than subvert the heuristic process of discovery.

Chapter 3

Definition: Heuristic

- **Encouraging discovery of solutions: relating to or using a method of teaching that encourages learners to discover solutions for themselves.**
- **May involve trial and error: using or arrived at by a process of trial and error rather than set rules.**
- **Able to change: can describe a computer software program that modifies itself in response to the varying conditions it encounters.**
- **Experience-based exploratory techniques for problem solving, learning, and discovery.**
- **A way to grow that does not involve rigid dogmatic, black-and- white requirements.**

So here, in the form of a heuristic approach, we have a method that can allow us to approach all issues in our lives, no matter how challenging they may seem at the onset. It does not ask you to believe anything, or to buy into anything. It simply suggests you "check it out," to observe and see where it leads, "as if" it were true. If it has value for you, either within a very specific focus, or offers a different perspective on a broader challenge, it is doing its job.

There is no guarantee anything suggested herein is going to work for YOU. They are powerful ideas that have worked for me and many others, and have been found helpful and empowering by clients in my counseling practice, workshops and seminars.

Try it and see if it works for you. This is the heuristic approach. No dogma, no rules, no doctrines. It's simply an opportunity to see if this approach holds value for you and if your life is more empowered as a result.

Chapter 4

The Simple Reality

"Our universal truth, now evident, is that we are co-creators in the universe. It is the alignment of our intention and the application of our "free" will and choice, aligned with that of the Source that forms the very core of all our creation. It is this uniquely creative conscious choice that is at the very heart of things...and is the simple truth, as well."

How would your life be different if you truly held that, "we are all the universe, connected through spirit, manifest through energy, moved through light, linked through Love...and we are just waking up to the true nature of our creative potential." (JS) It is not necessary to fully understand or to believe this statement in order to begin to check it out, or to begin to explore its effect on your life by applying it "as if true." You are using it then as a heuristic device to study and discover its value for you directly.

To simplify this process even further, try breaking the overall statement into simpler statements. For example, "Our universal truth, now evident, is that we are co-creators in the universe," may be the statement we choose to check against our experiences.

Its actual value lies not so much in believing it as in exploring its meaning and capability of generating new outcomes and solutions in our lives. Does it work for you as a way of living or a way of being and doing? Is it worth holding onto? Does it warrant further checking out as an idea?

Simply put, if this heuristic works for you in a way that improves your life or makes life better for you and leads to greater happiness, maybe it is a useful and productive way of experiencing things within and around you.

If something works for you and makes your life happier, healthier and more whole, it really doesn't matter how or why it works. It only matters that it works for you!

The chapters that follow are a goldmine for your heuristic exploration. Take nothing for granted. Above all do not get lulled into skipping the heuristic analysis. Each chapter's contents represent information I gathered and developed as part of my life process. It works for me, but the test is, whether it works for you. If something in particular jumps out at you, it is something you should particularly check out, as if true, to see if it works for you. If it doesn't, let it go and move on.

Chapter 5

Freedom of Choice

"We may all have the potential for free will, but we do not all have equal freedom, or equal freedom to choose. The primary instrument of choosing, our will, is anything but free. The tragic truth is that, in most cases, the will is so enslaved by our systems of belief that it may take lifetimes to set it free."

The notion that we are all equally free and all have an equal capacity to choose disregards the extreme degree to which our will is entangled in our conscious and unconscious perceptions, beliefs, culture and ego. If this were not the case, it would be relatively easy for all of us to view reality in pretty much the same way. "What is, is simply...what it is."

Our inability to accept the reality of "what is," exactly as it is, has led to the formation of an alternative to reality, based on a set of beliefs which pretend to hide the more frightening aspects of our reality. This gives rise to limiting mental constructs, such as the ego construct which provides the bedrock of our enslavement.

This bedrock is not only pervasive but forms the very basis of our culture of belief, and I refer to this as our ego's "conspiracy" because it is hidden. It controls us. We have no idea it is even happening, much less who the major players are. We don't know its agenda, how it works, or why it is even there. It pretends to hide all that frightens us in our world and purports to protect us from these jagged fears that lie just beneath the surface of our consciousness. In fact, beneath just about every belief we hold, lies a fear we have yet to accept. Fear is the very core of our ego's conspiracy!

It is incredibly limiting to live within the experiential confines of our fear and anxiety. We eventually become so limited that our will and our freedom of choice become enslaved by what we were/are unwilling and, as yet, unable to accept.

Let me repeat that. **It is incredibly limiting to live within the experiential confines of our fear and anxiety. We eventually become so limited that our will and our freedom of choice become enslaved by what we were and are unwilling and, as yet, unable to accept.** Thus, any situation which threatens us and generates fear and anxiety is either repressed or rendered unconscious. If there is enough dissonance, it becomes necessary for an alternate set of beliefs to be created and imposed on the actual reality in order to counteract this anxiety experience.

For example, if as a child we witness a tragic event which traumatizes, we may need to repress the experience or move it out of our conscious mind entirely. However, if it becomes too difficult, we may be forced to create a set of beliefs or use existing beliefs to explain it. For example, the belief that Hurricane Katrina was a punishment by God, for the evils of

America, was linked to everything from legalized abortion to Ellen DeGeneres.

Thus, we are not only enslaved by our limiting beliefs and what we cannot accept as reality, but we are also forced to operate on a set of beliefs that do not reflect the actual objective reality. It generates an illusion of reality rather than an actual experience of truth. This is, of course, a type of hiding and denial which, along with repression and other defense mechanisms, represent the first line of defense against anxiety and fear and are the primary tools of the ego. In fact, it becomes one of the earliest stages of our personal ego and can begin in the womb, at birth, or in the first few years of life. It will remain in control of our life, decision making and motivation, supposedly protecting us from fear until the conspiracy against our truth is revealed. As *A Course in Miracles* proclaims, **"Nothing real can be threatened. Nothing unreal exists. Herein lies the peace of God."**

Chapter 6

(For Heuristic Exploration)

Beliefs vs Knowing

"In the realm of time and space, the rational ego mind contains only beliefs. All beliefs are simply useful constructs and abstractions, not a true reality, but illusionary maps about reality. They are not themselves real, but rather our best guess about what reality is...or more to the point, what we need it to be. Our beliefs determine how we perceive a reality, and they stand as the mediator between actual reality and our experience of that reality."

What we experience is defined by what we believe. It reflects the whole role of our perception in our experience of reality. Thus, the more distorted our belief systems, the more distorted our perceptions. As our perception of reality grows more distorted, the more skewed our experience of reality becomes, and the further it exists from an objective reality.

A belief is the secondary or less immediate **condition of abstraction** in relation to a reality and **believing** is a necessary condition to sustain the illusion of reality. A belief is to be distinguished from knowing, which bears a real one-to-one relationship with an objective reality.

Knowing is the more **immediate condition of being** in relation to a reality. It is the experience of being one with the reality, without an intermediary stage of self-consciousness, perception or abstraction wherein there is a need to define, explain, order, organize, structure and understand it. Reality simply "is what is, as it is."

For most, there is only the perception of reality, which is to say that they exist in a world of illusion, filtered through the lens of their belief systems. They are not in touch with their direct knowing experience.

Until we are able to live in our **knowing** we are required to continue to explore and create beliefs which can serve to expand our perception of reality, and in so doing permit us to expand one step closer to **reality.**

So what has this difference between beliefs and knowing to do with anything? Simply put, it has everything to do with our experience of our own life. If we believe that we are a victim, based on experiences in our life and on the lives of our parents and other family members, it can be quite challenging to turn that belief into something positive. At this point, we have come to see a huge amount of evidence to support our belief, right?

It would take being willing to try another way. To dare to take some risks based on a different belief structure, at least in the beginning. Then, if it turns out to empower your life, it is experienced as a knowing, and no longer just a new belief. "I embrace all that supports my success in all things; I release all that would not fully support my empowerment." These are heuristic affirmations for you to check out and see if, over time, your life experience improves. When they are combined with adopting the new world view, that is to say, living your life as if the affirmations were true, then things slowly begin to change in your favor.

Now, it isn't necessary to process each individual belief. Maybe this has value at first, as we initially check out the value of some of our personal beliefs. Economy suggests there may be a better way once we are clear on the productivity of transforming our beliefs. A simple way to do this is to group beliefs into appropriate groups or categories.

Beliefs can be organized according to category. It is quite possible to organize them broadly into five key areas. For example:

Career: Beliefs about Status, Success, Failure, Survival, Self-Worth, and your future

Health: Beliefs about Energy, Wellness, Illness, Vitality, Weight, and your well-being

Finance: Beliefs about Money, Prosperity, Lack, Wealth, Loss, and its impact on you

Development: Beliefs about Personal, Social, Spiritual, Religious status quo

Relationships: Beliefs about Family, Partners, Friends, Society, and their value to you

These categories can be broken down still further into three areas. For example: **Survival** related beliefs, **Well-Being** related beliefs, and **Power** related beliefs. It is recommended at this point that you identify some of your basic level beliefs as specifically as you can. You can always group them later.

Ultimately, the heuristics can help you to examine your own beliefs and help you to begin to find your way home. Over time, the ultimate distinction between your beliefs, as instilled in you through your culture, family, and ego, and that which is your truth and who you truly are, **as determined by your own inner knowing,** will become clear.

Using the heuristics forms the basis in your taking the first step. Examining your beliefs and expanding your conscious understanding of how you are being held back by your limiting beliefs is next. Once these steps are completed you are ready to move on.

The chapters that follow are built on a foundation of true openness and an attitude of enquiry. The exploration of your authentic self, the healing of your ego's conspiracy, and the recognition of your relationships as a spiritual path is based upon your capacity for an open exploration of what will follow.

Chapter 7

Relationships and All Acts of Creation

"The act of creation is predictably challenging for most people. As a result, creations are often abandoned in the process of being created. This challenge exists because of the difficulty involved in overcoming the hurdles inherent in each of the 5 stages of creation. These hurdles must be transitioned by every creator, if there is to be the birth of a new creation. These stages accompany every act of creation including relationships, new projects, new ideas, inventions, partnerships and joint ventures, and especially the higher expressions of love."

All of our life is, to some extent, about relationship, whether we are talking about relationship to ourselves, our partners, family, lovers and significant others in our life, or even non-significant others. Indeed, we are in a relationship with our thoughts and ideas, body, health, career, finances, jobs, businesses and all of our creations regardless of the nature of the project.

Given this reality, it is interesting how little we actually know about what goes on in a relationship of any kind. It strikes me as quite odd that we know so little, given that we are all involved in so many relationships. It is, I believe, a statement of the human condition that our knowledge of our relationships is so limited.

Some might believe that we don't particularly need to know anything about relationships. For example, corporations, sports teams, NASA projects all have been very successful presumably without this knowledge. It is, however, entirely possible that these are more a reflection of a capable and knowledgeable leadership and the presence of a clear and well defined vision.

If, in fact, capable and knowledgeable leadership is present, both the vision and the key elements of relationship become clearly evident, both embodied in the leadership and also in how individual team members exemplify these embodiments. Yet, in the absence of this leadership and vision, the individual members do not fare as well. Thus, each member would ultimately benefit greatly from awareness, understanding, internalizing and applying the key elements of relationship. In this way, decentralization of an organization is able to more fully empower the members and, thus, the organization and permit greater growth even in the absence of a specific focus on leadership.

There are very clearly defined stages of relationship and they follow very clear patterns of projection (subconscious positive or negative judgments externalized onto others, to deny the reality of them being true about one's self).

STAGE 1 – HONEYMOON:(Positive projections)

Jen, an attractive 23 year old client, has a new man in her life. Although she has only just recently met him, she is absolutely certain "he is the right man for me." Jen advises, "He is different, and we are most certainly soul mates." This is the third "Mr. Right," in about a year and a half. She came to see me initially to help her get over a previous relationship that had not worked out. These relationships always begin well but typically within about a 6 month period she is distraught because either he has left her, or she has left him. Of course, no amount of caution can dissuade her from going full tilt into the new relationship or even to slow down a bit, especially in the earliest few weeks. Jen believes that he has to be the right one, because all of the signs are there. He calls her almost every day. He is generous, caring, sensitive but strong, handsome, bright, and doing well financially. He proclaims his love for her and, "Oh yes, the sex is terrific." Is it possible she has really found the right man? Yes, it is possible, but it's not likely, based on Jen's pattern in relationships. She lives for the romance, and when things begin to change, it always seems to catch her by surprise, and she is left wondering how she could have missed "all that about him."

Alas, Jen, the first stage of relationship is more illusion than anything that corresponds to actual reality. That is why we refer to it as the HONEYMOON Stage or the ROMANCE Stage of relationship. Everything is just peachy, just as we had hoped, because we are not in a real relationship. It is about having found Mr./Mrs. Right, the ideal job, the right project to showcase our skills, etc. These are very real to us but do not reflect a full picture of what we have chosen.

This stage can last for days, weeks or months depending on how many partners, projects, jobs, etc. we have had. Most people prefer this stage to any other, even though it isn't real, because it is so dramatic, filled with such promise and incredible feelings of all that we have idealized. It offers to give us all we've ever hoped for. That is why it is so difficult for Jen to accept any other reality than the one she is now projecting and any discussion to the contrary is viewed as very negative.

It is our idealized relationship projected onto our partner. It isn't real, but at this point we are so certain that it is real and will last forever, that we go into a kind of denial about our partner and particularly about his/her potential faults. **Make no mistake about it, everyone has a dark side, and it is usually hidden.** This is not, however, what is shown at the very beginning of our relationships. Even when we do share some perspective on it, it is denied in order to maintain the illusion of "rightness."

It is difficult for Jen and most people to see the projection, much less own it. It can seem like their partner is "this one way" and that's all there is to it. For Jen, that one way is in perfect alignment with her projection. It may even be that the partner is a good fit for what Jen is projecting. However, it is almost certain that it does not include the alter ego or dark side of the partner, and as such this becomes one of the key problems in bringing about the end of the relationship. In Jen's case, it is only a few weeks into the relationship when the initial cracks begin to show and that initiates a painful period of conflict and struggle.

STAGE 2 – POWER STRUGGLE: (Negative Projections)

There was no actual full reality to Jen's projections and they only covered what she wanted to see. They did not take the reality, as a whole, into account. When the darker side of things begins to surface and the original picture begins to get murky, we can't imagine we were so wrong about our partner. For Jen, this almost always comes as a surprise, and even though it has happened to her before, it always seems to come unexpectedly and then she feels blindsided. "You just can't trust men..." is her new phrase.

Discoveries of another side to our partner that we don't care for, or a series of issues that turn out to make our job very restrictive, or our project continually having to be reworked to the point it no longer bears any resemblance to the original, come as a shock. For Jen, these are experienced as heartbreaks and rather than feel the pain associated with these heartbreaks, she would rather fight it out, engage in conflict and power struggle, to prove that the fault for this is not in any way hers. It rests with her partner (boss, or project director). As it happens, this stage is rampant with projections as well. All of our deepest fears about us begin to emerge and these become the fuel that feeds our dark projections. We cannot own this. This is a very painful period in our relationships and high levels of intensity and desperation replace the previous feelings of love, hope, excitement and promise.

Occasionally, this intensity will overflow and spill over in places that are not appropriate for such drama. It can happen with a partner at a party, a restaurant, in public, creating embarrassment and stress for everyone present. The conflict becomes unmanageable and soon escalates into a power struggle. The honeymoon-romance is over. It is now about deciding who is at fault, who is to blame, how each was deceived, who will be the victim and who the aggressor, who will feel all the feelings and who will become detached and shut down emotionally. For Jen, this was all quite predictable and even discussed in session, but the lure of the romance proved stronger than reality. At this stage, Jen's relationship is in trouble, designed to hide heartbreak and vulnerability. It can't continue on this way, so it is either commit or quit.

STAGE 3 – COMMIT OR QUIT: (DEAD ZONE)

It is at this stage in the relationship that a true choice needs to be made whether to stay in the relationship with our partner, (project, job, creation), or move on. The volatility and painful conflicts cannot continue to escalate in the explosive manner they have been occurring. For Jen, this point signals it is time to go. "There is no love left, and I don't want to live this way." And, though this isn't quite true, it feels that way for Jen...it is time to begin the cycle again.

I recall leaving a relationship and asking myself on the way out the door how much love I still had for my former partner. The internal answer was 4%, so I slammed the door extra hard, as if to say, "It's your fault I no longer love you." The truth is, the love wasn't gone. It had been layered over with so much hidden resentment, judgments and unfulfilled expectations and projections, that 96% of it was no longer accessible. It was still there but buried under a mountain of rubble, all that remained of our former relationship.

Sometimes, people choose to remain in the relationship in an attempt to salvage what was left. There can be a variety of reasons for this that have nothing to do with love but with security, embarrassment, money, status quo, etc. What then follows is that the negative feelings, bitterness and resentments, volatility and lavish outbursts need to be contained.

What this amounts to is a closing down of feelings so that the experience of them is contained and repressed. When this happens, we are unable to feel much of anything. The relationship is more stable but at the price of feeling. You can see this sometimes between couples that have been together for a while. They rarely communicate, except for the occasional few sounds, and they basically ignore each other. This is why it is often referred to as the Dead Zone, and mirrors the absence of understanding as to what is actually happening in terms of projections.

For a few, there is a real desire to release and share the actual love that is present, and it is here that the first real stage of non-projection begins.

STAGE 4 – THE EMPOWERMENT OPTION:

Following the Dead Zone, for those who choose to commit and not close themselves down, a new and more daring option emerges. This is an option so radical and unusual that it has been literally unthinkable. That option is to simply own all of the problems generated by the projections **as our own.** This really is unthinkable, right? Our Ego rebels at the thought! "What do you mean I take all the blame?" "You've got to be kidding!" "Let him get away with that? No way!" "I wasn't the one who..." and, so the reaction carries on and on.

I heard a story about Chuck Yeager and his efforts to break the sound barrier. This barrier had stood since the beginning of flight and even though in theory it was possible to break the barrier, none had officially accomplished this feat. As the story goes, when the sound barrier was approached, the planes would begin to shake and vibrate. As a result, almost all pilots would ease up and back off. Yeager, instead of slowing in the midst of the shaking, accelerated and actually moved through the sound barrier. He was on the other side of a barrier that, in spite of existing technology, fear and ignorance held in place. Regardless of the actual authenticity of this story, Yeager did something the others had not done, and that was to push through a place where he had to overcome his fear and the response to try and save himself.

So, in actual fact, it is the counter logical response that we are proposing. That, in fact, we take full responsibility for the key issues that are problematic. Now there is good news and bad news here. The good news is that we become more personally empowered by reclaiming our projections and can actually rise above these limitations because we have taken back the power for change. We no longer have to wait for things to change outside of us. The bad news is we can no longer blame each other. In the example I gave earlier about slamming the door as I left, we began to communicate, actually own our projections and while it took quite a long while, we did work it out and forgive each other, even though it was not about the other person.

In the face of this, many choose to continue to blame, thus leaving themselves powerless to change and/or keep the relationship alive. This is a hard place to be, and yet what we know is that this is a clear case of blind projection and expectations that have obscured a hidden darkness within us, and we continue to repeat the pattern until we see it and own it.

Stage 4 is the first stage of real relationship and of empowered relationship. It is empowered because we can take back our projections and own them as our creation. At first, it's hard to recognize that they are not so much a picture of our partner as they are a reflection of our own hidden mind. Sure, our partner may have been a good screen on which to project our hidden mind, but the important thing is that we own these and begin to see what was going on in our unconscious that caused us to dump our projections on the other person in the first place.

If we repress or dump stuff we can't deal with in the unconscious mind, it forces the mind to project it outward so that we begin to deal with it. It is the only way our mind can call us to address what is not real in order to restore what is real. Like the sound barrier, it exists as a limit that awaits our willingness to move forward.

This can take a while as we struggle to own our projections but wind up falling back into old disempowering patterns of projection and blame. It is a trial and error thing for a long while until we really get used to seeing the truth in it and begin to apply it in all areas of our life. It is one of the most intriguing heuristics, and I invite you to check it out. It may just save your relationships.

For those who are determined enough and persistent enough, a new level of creative mastery emerges permitting you to have the relationships you have longed for all your life.

STAGE 5 – CO-CREATIVE RELATIONSHIP:

For those who have remained true to their heart's vision of partnership, this last stage is the culmination of all the work that has gone before. The honeymoon stage returns, only this time released of all the projections and discord. The romance, as well, returns but without the intense drama.

This stage is about integration and actualization of a co-creative dynamic that does not require all of the conflict and struggle. It is possible to work in an objective way with others, especially your partner, your project team members and fellow employees.

Co-creativity with the Source now becomes possible. As projections are lifted and connection with your true vision and purpose realign again with Source, they become one in the service of creation.

This is the point of all relationships, to find your way back to the truth of who you are, why you are here, and to align and serve with your co-creative partners in the manifestation of Sacred Creation.

As it turns out, this can be a bit of a rarity on this planet, but as more and more people are responding to the call of their heart, and as they begin to understand the true underlying dynamics and guiding principles of relationship, they begin to move forward with others in the ultimate vision of creating heaven on earth.

Nothing could be richer or more rewarding than being in this co-creative adventure with everyone else way out on the leading edge of creation. If you are in this place at this time, it is not an accident! It is because you chose it long before you entered time and space, before your starry journey first began... shine on bright light!

Thus, at each stage of relationship we are confronted by whether we are going to choose our beliefs about relationships, or learn a deeper truth. Our relationship beliefs are driven by and defended by our ego. Whether it is in the form of our pride, control, fear, our ego is at work, ostensibly to protect us, but actually blocking our path to truth and the deeper experience of our own being. That's the bad news! The good news is it offers us a profound opportunity to grow in truth.

Using the medium of our relationship as a spiritual path presents a whole new perspective on growing in our truth as we take ownership of our projections and invite our partner to do the same. As we do this, it not only helps to unfold the many illusions we are living under, but strengthens the relationship and sets both our self and our partner free from our most limiting and stifling projections.

Chapter 8

(For Heuristic Exploration)

Change Your Mind & Change Your Life: The Choice to Live!

> "The great tragedy of living is not death or dying...it is living your life as if you were already dead!"

> "Some might be surprised to discover just how many people are willing to sentence themselves to a life of limitation, psychic and personal poverty, enslavement to what is untrue, and then ultimately, a death of the spirit. This is the greatest sadness of all,that they have no permission to be who they really are."

Surprising things happen every day. They not only happen in secret faraway places. They happen all around you. Beyond the physical world that you can see, beyond your thoughts and emotions, there exists another world, a world of pure potential, a place where anything and everything is possible.

I was getting my hair cut the other day and chatting with the owner. He told me about how struck he was by the differences in people's reactions to his invitation to go to a fundraiser.

The invitation was an opportunity to have a "micro adventure" just outside of the comfort zone. Only a few perceived the value in this invitation, just for its own sake. He was troubled at how many conditions people placed on participating in their own life.

A key question here is, "What do people perceive differently that creates such a different response for each individual?" Some may see it as just a money grab, while others see an opportunity to contribute to a worthy cause. Some may perceive their energy is just too low to go out, especially after working all day, while still others see an opportunity to raise their energy through being out and about with other people.

Whatever the case, it is an opportunity missed, a chance to examine the beliefs you hold that determine your life experience. It is your chance, regardless of your perceptions and choices, to participate in your own life in a more meaningful and conscious way. There is, of course, no right or wrong choice. There is only that choice that improves, or does not improve your life. You can change your life by daring to live it on purpose, based on what you know in your own soul to be true.

If you are too certain that your present **unexamined** life is right, then you leave no option to explore other ways of experiencing your life. If you have done your exploratory work and decide your previous life is right for you, then you are "blessed." Either way, you have the opportunity to change your life for the better.

An article exploring the theme of "passive suicide" speculates that as many as 80-90% of all deaths are "passive suicides." What exactly is this phenomenon? Passive suicide is literally suicide by giving up on what is deepest in us to give, and by not participating fully in our life. It may look like an accident, or a serious illness, or being in the wrong place at the wrong (right?) time, but the deeper truth is that a point has been reached in life where someone could not move forward any longer. They could not, or were unwilling to, take their next step. To put it another way, they had given up. They had unconsciously lost their "desire to live with passion and purpose." This is not necessarily true for anyone in particular, living or dead, nor is any of us in a position to judge. It is a trend that has been noted, and that's all. Take note, however, of decisions you may or may not be making, and whether they add or detract from your life.

Was it the absence of a dynamic vision, or a purpose or mission that inspired and uplifted them? Or perhaps, it had more to do with a fear of the unknown consequences of such a next step, of what it would mean to surrender another level of predictability or control in their life. Maybe, in an unconscious way, they were drawn into the elaborate conspiracy of the ego. Perhaps, so much so that it became more difficult or even inconceivable to respond to anything except by physically withdrawing from life. This is a denial of life, and a decision that it would be easier to let go of a deeper expression of your present life than take the next step forward towards embracing it fully.

I recently had the opportunity to experience this in an up close and personal way. Generally speaking, over the last decade or so, I had been "slowly withdrawing" from an active involvement in my life, my workshops, seminars and empowerment counseling practice. I had an awesome and inspiring student I was mentoring and a handful of "select clients" I saw on a regular basis. I felt like, and even commented that, "my work here is done." I made myself believe it, even though there was a very strong, insistent part of me that longed to live more, love more, share more, and contribute more.

I comforted myself with, "Look, I don't think anybody really wants to see any more of you, much less see you as a credible representative of any kind of empowerment. You are overweight, you do not exercise at all, and everything you do seems to require a massive effort."

Periodically, I made some feeble efforts to write this little book and when that was unsuccessful, I decided to turn it all over to the student I was mentoring. "Yep," I thought, "that's the ticket!"

The insistent part of me kept asking if this was it for me. Of course, I didn't answer. I just stocked up more on cookies and cakes and commented to myself, "I must be experiencing a kind of Buddha consciousness."

Chapter 9

Paradise Lost – Paradise Regained

"No one saves us but ourselves. No one can
and no one may. We ourselves must walk the
path." Buddha

In truth, I had reached a place where I was unwilling to move forward in my life. Time passed; one, two, three months, then four months. Summer passed and fall moved in. The insistent part of me continued to ask **if this was it for me**. Each time I did not answer, but I did less and less. I had basically given up on writing.

My routine each day was the same, unbelievably, boringly, depressingly, the same. I would trade currencies, and then I would watch the Discovery Channel, Documentary Channel, History Channel. I watched several documentary programs on the ghosts of people who had died, and how these people didn't realize they were dead. Most just wandered through the same routine every day, never varying it. I began to wonder about myself. Is it possible I had died and didn't realize it? I certainly felt dead, both metaphorically and literally. Laugh if you will, but there was an engaging kind of logic to it all, and I seemed to fit the pattern.

Still, the insistent part of me, with its question, would not go away. Then I got the bright idea of hiring a ghostwriter to do the book for me. Pretty fitting, I thought. This will shut that part up, and maybe then I can have some peace. Following a brief search, I settled on a likely candidate and we began to email back and forth. In one of the emails, following a discussion of how we would collaborate, it basically dawned on me that even if someone else was to write the book, I would still need to know, explain and communicate all that needed to be shared. I would still need to address all that was holding me back, even if just to have someone else write it for me.

As I thought about it, I questioned whether it even needed to be written. Why would I even bother with such an endeavor? What is such a big deal, anyway?

Then it struck me that **this was what I had been preparing for, it was my Calling...my gift to give to the world.** Nobody else could or would write this book. "Okay, I get it...this was my next step...and here I was busy trying to delegate it. What a funny guy I am." I had just made the discovery that had eluded me for so long. I started to feel better and better and began to write.

As I began, I became more and more excited. The opportunity to engage in a process of discovery and to potentially be of value again began to awaken within me. I felt, what I refer to as the "Magic Elixir" again, the flow of spirit uplifting and illuminating my soul and body.

Adults, like children, thrive on discovery. It is the "magic elixir" that flows through them, inviting them to grow, learn, explore, expand and develop. Only when fear begins to enter the picture does our flow begin to diminish and along with it our creativity, openness, love and connection.

In essence, we have found our next step, and it is generating survival concerns for our ego, with which of course we are identified. In truth, the next step does not generate anything except excitement and discovery for the higher aspects of our nature, but for the ego it creates major fears or, the great fears, as they are called. Thus, when the fear of the next step is greater than the perceived consequences of not moving forward, we have hit a place where the vitality of life, the life energy, magic elixir is unable to flow.

In this place, due to the presence of the ego's great fears, it may not be possible for us to move forward alone, without some kind of Grace. For some, this blockage can last for very long periods of time, perhaps even lifetimes. For others, there is the presence of a Gift, a Grace, a Guide that can reduce and/ or eliminate the ego blockage. That is the highest vision for this book, that it serve as a Gift of Grace for anyone needing or desiring to move forward in their life.

Chapter 10

Greatness and the Great Fears

"In order to reach our Greatness we must first address the source of our limitations and resistance. This involves facing the core of our ego conspiracy and the 'great fears' that surround it. This is what ultimately prepares us for Greatness, our ability to face and overcome all that would oppose our emergence."

There are many types of fear that emanate from deep within the core of our ego. These fears range from the basic types, such as physical survival in the presence of imminent danger, to learned fears, such as in public speaking, all the way to the great fears. The former basic fears are not what we mean when we speak of the great fears. These basic fears are part of our physiological survival mechanisms, hardwired in, and are intended to protect the survival of the body from potential threats perceived to be in the environment. This is the classic fight or flight response.

On the other hand, we have the great fears, which are part of the ego's survival mechanism. They are keyed to the psychic survival of the ego. Anything that might be perceived as a threat to the ego or its survival is reacted to with great fear and steps are taken to block or eliminate the perceived threat.

These great fears are designed to protect the ego against the fact that it is not real, and that its very nature is an illusion, a construct, which derives its illusory nature from people's willingness to believe in it. We know that no amount of defense can protect what is unreal from the inevitable truth of what is real. Yet it tries to hold onto its place with those who would perceive it as real. More than that, it has woven an elaborate plan to keep us small and to attempt to hide our Greatness from us. I call this worshipping in the church of Rev. Small or Rev. Little, and this plan is at the heart of the conspiracy against our "knowing". This is where we find the sabotage, the plots to keep us limited, and to keep us unaware of our True Greatness. Even though the ego is unreal, it uses the illusion of reality, so it has been dubbed the Reverend. (No slight intended toward church, clergy or the name Small or Little).

Thus, if we are aware of the truth of what is real, even a little, the ego begins to slowly deflate like a tire with a slow leak. The ego employs its lines of defense, the great fears, and its psychic hold on us based on its firsthand knowledge of our deepest shames and humiliations, to try and deter any further exploration. It may even work for a while, even a long while, but sooner or later, because it is not real, it loses any control it had over us.

Each of us has internalized the key imperatives of the ego in the form of deep psychic fears, the great fears. We have been conditioned through our experience of these fears, and a culture rooted in them, to avoid at all costs these areas specifically.

The problem for the ego is that each level of fear that is exposed as a lie exposes a deeper level still and this leads to the next level of potential exposure. Thus, for the ego this represents the basic dismantling of its fear-based Conspiracy.

Make no mistake about it, the ego has a strong hold on each of us. Yet, how can what is unreal cause us any problem? What is needed then is to expose the illusion for exactly what it is, an illusion.

Chapter 11

The Ego's Five Great Fears

"Each step, no matter how difficult, is ours
to take. The most important step is always the
first, and the next first, and the next first."

So, what are the ego's Five Great Fears? Ranging from the lowest
(5) to the highest (1):

5. **Awareness** of our Truth! (Objective Nature of our Reality).

4. **Participation** in Life! (Openly, Objectively, Fully Present).

3. **Accountability** for our Life! (Full Responsibility for our
Creations).

2. **Acceptance** of our core of darkness! (Separation, Exposure,
Shame).

1. **Embracing** our Truth, Greatness, Light! (Innocence, Vision,
Love).

Each level of fear is, of course, driven by the ego in its effort to keep us from knowing and being who we really are. Each level of fear is intended to stall going on to the next level. Each level of exploration triggers the ego's conspiracy of fear against our knowing who we really are.

I am reminded of Plato's Analogy of the Cave, wherein prisoners are chained to a wall for the whole of their lives. They can see only shadows that are created by a fire behind them. They believe these shadows to be real. They have so fully accepted the belief that this is the reality, that it creates great fear for them when the suggestion is made that there is more.

When one person escapes and tries to share with them the truth of his discoveries within and beyond the cave, they would rather attack him than face and experience the truth. This can be seen as characteristic of the levels of fear that are activated when people's fundamental beliefs are challenged. The attempt, on the part of the prisoners, is to remain unaware, in hiding and denial, because they would have to face their **ego's fifth greatest fear of being aware of objective Truth, beyond the cave,** especially their own Truth. Awareness of this objective reality is where all freedom begins.

Further, the natural desire to be involved with others triggers the **ego's fourth greatest fear of our participation** with others and community. As with external cult leaders, and the ego as Reverend Small, there is the presence of a resistance to our full participation with others. This is one of the early signs of a cult: the separation of the individual from their family and community. This fear may come across in our experience as a toxic anticipation of public shame and a palpable fear of being exposed, humiliated, and embarrassed, especially if it is in front of others.

The desire to blame others appears to offer a degree of comfort, especially if it saves us from having to take responsibility for our thoughts, feelings and actions. Thus, any movement in the direction of greater accountability is not going to be met with ego approval. If we are taking a high level of responsibility, ego recognizes it won't be long before we no longer need Reverend Small. The **ego's third greatest fear of accountability** becomes activated and we actively engage in a denial of our responsibility and accountability. If others are to blame, **then we will never become empowered** because we will be forever waiting for others to accept their blame, thus vindicating us. The challenge here is that we have placed the power for growth and change outside of us, rather than within. So, we have good news and bad news. If we have the power for change within us, we are free to take any step we wish to take without needing anything from the outside. We are empowered. That's good news! The bad news is that we can no longer blame, or we are right back where we were.

The **ego's second greatest is the fear of our darkness** and seems to be one of the most difficult for all of us to deal with. It carries the sum of the fear energy of all the other fears. It is the cumulative core of all that we don't want to know about and certainly don't want others to know about. It carries the energy of life and death and is the core of our perception of ourselves as dark, unworthy and evil. There is the potential of so believing this dark picture that we may be tempted to act on it. This is a good place to ask for and find support for your journey through this level. There is no more truth to it than any other level. It is an illusion appearing real!

The ultimate fear we face is not what we might expect. The **ego's first, highest and greatest fear is the fear of our own Greatness.** The ego recognizes that once we begin to access our own truth, its days are numbered. The plot and conspiracy are over. The only choice at this point for the ego is to surrender in the service of the Soul.

I remember my very first public presentation on this topic entitled, "Emergence to Greatness." I had made all the preparations and anticipated probably about 12-15 people attending. I had made some notes to permit me to stay on track and was just about to look them over. I was in a room adjacent to the presentation room. I decided I would look out to see if any of the seats were filling up. To my absolute shock there were 75-80 people present.

I began to hyperventilate and experience a huge sense of panic. This was no ordinary experience for me. I was accustomed to public speaking, having made dozens of presentations over the years. This was sheer panic. I thought, "Oh my God!" and tried to look at my notes. They meant absolutely nothing. Greek would have made more sense at that time. Meanwhile, my panic and terror continued to grow.

I thought, "For God's sake get a grip," as my panic grew into terror. It was about five minutes until presentation time, and I am hearing, "There is no way that I'm going out there." It was unbearable. I seriously began to entertain the thought of a nervous breakdown as a way out of this impossible situation.

One of the support staff came in to alert me that it was almost time to go on. My fear was so great and so intense that he could feel it radiating across the room. He turned instantly and left. I was truly in a mess and literally had my back against the wall separating me from the group. I noticed an Exit sign and a door leading to the outside. I thought to myself, "I will just leave through the Exit door." At that point I caught a glimpse in my mind of headlines which read, "Emergence to Greatness Speaker chooses not to emerge and exits through a side door!"

There was something so funny about that I began to laugh uncontrollably until I was almost in tears.

By the time of the official presentation, as I was being introduced, the fear had all but abated. The notes still made no sense, but I was relaxed enough to go ahead without them. They were a distraction from the quality of "loving connection" I began to feel as the presentation went on. It was a huge success, and I felt very blessed to have had the opportunity to share with these people.

It was about whether I would/could choose to accept the honor and blessing of being there for others. The experience of Love and Connection that emerged that night has not diminished over the years, except for the few times when I have been frightened to take my next step.

I just needed to release my sense of self-conscious smallness in order to permit the direct flow of my Greatness and my connectedness with all Greatness...to pass it on and to give it to others. As Marianne Williamson wrote:

> **"It serves no one for any of us to remain small. It is our destiny to be fully who we are... to be Great. The true act of arrogance is to hide our giftedness and creativity and live these little lives of quiet desperation." - Marianne Williamson**

> **"Our deepest fear is not that we are inadequate. Our deepest fear is that we are powerful beyond measure. It is our light, not our darkness that most frightens us. We ask ourselves, 'Who am I to be brilliant, gorgeous, talented, fabulous?' Actually, who are you not to be? You are a child of God. Your playing**

small does not serve the world. There is nothing enlightened about shrinking so that other people won't feel insecure around you. We are all meant to shine, as children do. We were born to make <u>manifest</u> the glory of God that is within us. It's not just in some of us; it's in everyone. And as we let our own light shine, we unconsciously give other people permission to do the same. As we are liberated from our own fear, our presence automatically liberates others." – Marianne Williamson.

Chapter 12

Introduction to Heuristic Triangle Graphic

The triangle graphic that follows, symbolizes the relationship between the higher spiritual realm (the Upper Triangle) and the earthly realm of the ego (the Lower Triangle). It conveys the relationship between the realms and the nature of our calling, to rise above the limits inherent in the lower triangle in order to express our True Being and Greatness.

In the Middle Area (the Workshop Area), lies the gap that must be crossed in order to lay claim to our true point of Greatness (corner). Simple enough, but not easy at all because of the pull of the Lower Triangle, controlled by the ego and its conspiracy of limitation, (which is where we find ourselves).

Each of the corners of the Lower Triangle is represented by a point. This point, however, is just the tip of the iceberg, and it is only as we begin to look more closely that we begin to discover how deep the conspiracy runs. Each point is filled with a different set of fears, and even more than fear, deep feelings of panic and terror.

This **is not you or your truth**. It belongs to your ego (and its experience) as you begin to move in the direction of the Higher Triangle. Since in most cases we do not distinguish between the experience of our ego and our true natural experience, we have no way of determining what originates with our ego and what the experience of our own Authentic Being is. We see it as all the same.

The purpose of the Heuristic triangles is to begin to map the terrain here. It can be used diagnostically to allow us to see more clearly how/where we are stuck, and as a healing tool to find the direction out (arrows), which is always the direction of our Higher Calling.

The Middle workshop area is where we must find the courage to begin our work. As said before it is not an easy matter, and yet it all begins with taking the first step, and then our next first step. The reason you are encouraged to utilize Heuristic approaches throughout, is so that you can become clearer and stronger on this journey, which only you can take to your true calling.

> **"I must be willing to give up what I am in
> order to become what I will be."**
>
> **Albert Einstein**

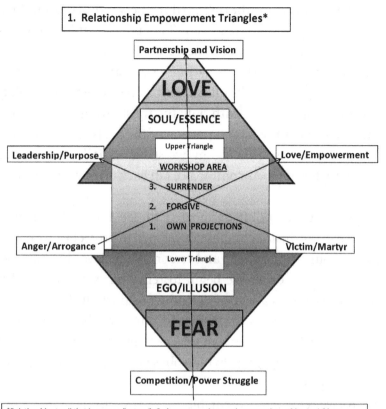

1. Relationship Empowerment Triangles*

Partnership and Vision

LOVE

SOUL/ESSENCE

Upper Triangle

Leadership/Purpose | Love/Empowerment

WORKSHOP AREA

3. SURRENDER

2. FORGIVE

1. OWN PROJECTIONS

Anger/Arrogance | Victim/Martyr

Lower Triangle

EGO/ILLUSION

FEAR

Competition/Power Struggle

*Relationships to all that is seen as "not me": God, cosmos, universe, planets, nations, cities, neighbors, partners, friends, enemies, lovers, family, health, career, employers, projects, all objects and all creations.

We are always in some form of relationship, whether that be with some aspect of our ego self, our partner, our lover, our siblings, our friends, our job, our creativity, our projects, our Higher Self, Soul, Spirit or Source.

The Triangles are a heuristic device designed to assist us with gaining more clarity around what is happening in our relationships, and to assess our unique point of view. We may or may not agree on our politics, religion, ideologies, but one thing is quite clear, our emotional experiences are always unique to us.

We strive to always be right, as do those we are in relationships with. This, of course, creates conflict and as conflict increases we tend to fall back on our "default style," our typical style of relating in a relationship. Anytime we are striving to prove our point – that we are right - it isn't just a one-dimensional point; it's like a huge iceberg with only the tip showing. Underneath the water line is the largest portion of the mass, totally unseen and unconscious. This is why we strive initially to be right. When that is not forthcoming, we fall back on our default style of relating.

Each corner point designated in the Lower Triangle is unique to our history and has developed to protect us from the pain of our primary fear and terror. We believe this has and will help us to cope. We begin to relive our story and faulty style of coping as a way of defending against all that we have projected onto our relationship. In other words, we begin to unconsciously reject our own unacceptable attributes by simply ascribing (projecting) them onto objects or persons in the world outside of us.

As we see our unacceptable attributes outside of ourselves and are willing to own and decode these projections as ours, we begin to heal our conspiracy and our relationships.

In the **Lower Triangle,** we see the **untrue masculine** corner characterized by arrogance, attack and abuse. The **untrue feminine** corner is characterized by victim, martyr and helplessness. The **competition** corner is a mix of the above two corners and characterized by power struggle, conflict and competition. This is in order to compensate for the perception of lack, and in order to stay away from being polarized to the other two corners.

Chapter 13

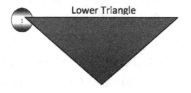

Lower Triangle

1. <u>Arrogance and Oppression</u>

Untrue Masculine

Style: Anger Attack, Denial
Fear: Anonymity
Terror: Nothingness, Non-Being
Compensation: Tantrum
Quote: "I am right that I am right."
Ego Belief: "I am better than others!"

The ego's Arrogance and Oppression corner is most typically seen as the reflection of the Untrue Masculine, whether the individual is male or female. It is characterized by a predisposition to anger and attack as its predominant style of interaction when the ego is under threat. It is where most people, male and female, go when they feel afraid. It is ready to fight in order to avoid an experience of being a victim. It usually involves attack, either verbally or physically.

This ego's great fear is being made to feel unimportant, invisible, or anonymous. Nothing could be worse for it! The Untrue Masculine actually feels it would truly cease to exist in any meaningful way if this happened. Everything is an accessory designed to show off the ego in its best light, including relationships.

When the ego is in this corner, and doesn't get its way the person can tantrum, rage and generally carry on badly. They like to be right, and in fact they insist on it. They are convinced that they are better than others and this leads to a high level of arrogance. In actual fact, it hides deep levels of fear based in a concern around their resistance to being the same as everyone else, as opposed to being larger than life. For these individuals, male or female, there is only fight, since flight is not an option. It fits the basic stereotype of the unevolved male.

A word of caution: These descriptions are somewhat extreme for the purposes of highlighting the characteristics of this corner of the Lower Triangle. In truth, we all spend some time here, and it is only a primary corner if it is our ego's predominant style (default style) of dealing with stress and threat. Most people would prefer to avoid the Victim and Martyr corner because of the negatives associated with it.

Josh, Arrogance and Oppression, The Untrue Masculine

Josh is a 28 year old equities trader who came to see me about quitting smoking. He had been smoking since he was in his teens and had a 2-pack a day habit. He was tall, with striking features and a gruff, abrupt, impatient personality.

He told me he had a low tolerance for frustration, which became evident as we began to explore the nature of his addiction. I had advised him that it would be pointless to see him until the underlying dynamics of his addiction began to surface, which usually begins to occur within a few days of stopping smoking. I suggested he try quitting for a week before his next appointment.

He called to see me ahead of his scheduled appointment time, saying it was urgent that he see me. I managed to get him in for a session and it was obvious he was agitated. I said that this was not unusual because smoking is often used to buffer and mask anger. I explained that the reason for not "using" for a period before the session was to allow the underlying dynamics and feelings to surface for healing.

He suddenly sat up in frustration and said, "You don't seem to realize that if I could stop smoking by myself I wouldn't be here." His face was red, flushed with anger. I acknowledged the kind of "Catch 22" factor; he was here to quit smoking and yet he has to quit smoking to be here. I acknowledged his plight and that it had obviously served its purpose. The anger and rage he was feeling was the first stage of what he was trying to cover up with smoking. I shared this with him and that this was exactly what he wanted to get to. He settled just a bit as I asked about his marital status.

"Divorced," he scowled.

"What happened?" I asked.

"Uhhh, we were fighting all the time...and she was a major bitch," he said. "She just wouldn't shut up and that caused me to get angry!"

"So, it was her fault that you divorced?" I asked.

He looked at me and his eyes narrowed slightly in a squint.

"Yes," he replied.

"Do you see her at all now?" I inquired.

He hesitated a moment. "Bitch got a restraining order."

"Are you in a relationship now?" I asked.

"No, and what the hell does that have to do with my quitting smoking?"

"A lot," I replied. "You use smoking to try and deaden your feelings, especially anger. You use anger to try to control and intimidate others, am I right?" There was no reply. "What do you do if that doesn't work?" I asked.

"I get angrier," he replied.

"And how is that working for you, especially in your relationships with women?" He looked away.

"How long have you been angry?" I asked Josh.

He grimaced, "Since I was a teenager."

"And what was happening in your life around then?"

"That was when my parents split and I went to live with my Dad. I hated that!"

"Why?" I asked.

"He was never there and I was on my own all the time. That was when I started to get in trouble stealing cars, doing B&E's and selling drugs, until I got caught. I was pretty lucky and got off with community service because it was just a possession charge. They didn't know about the other stuff, but it sure enough scared me. It was around this time that I started smoking big time."

We talked a bit further, on a very practical level, about his taking an anger management program to help him take responsibility for his anger. We would then deal with the underlying elements that precipitated the experience of his anger and arrogance.

This was a huge step for Josh. We continued to explore the key elements in his development. One huge piece came when he saw how angry he was at God. He felt that God had not been there for him and had in fact totally ignored him and his pain and suffering. This led to the first major breakthrough as he began a forgiveness process which would eventually extend to his parents and even his ex-wife.

There is still work for Josh to accomplish, including his learning to deal with his fears and feelings of being ignored. The primary thing Josh has going for him is that he actually did become a non-smoker, though there were a couple of setbacks along the way, and a bit of a relapse with the anger. But he continues to own his projections and to forgive as soon as he sees he is off the mark. No one can realistically ask for more than that.

Chapter 14

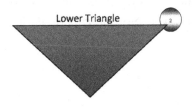

Lower Triangle

---

2. Victim and Martyr

Untrue Feminine

Style: Depression, Withdrawal, Hiding
Fear: Exposure
Terror: Guilt and Shame
Compensation: Sacrifice
Quote: "I am right that you are wrong."
Ego Belief: "I am worse than others!"

The ego's Victim and Martyr corner is seen as a reflection of the Untrue Feminine, whether or not the individual involved is male or female. It is typically characterized by feelings of depression and a desire to withdraw and hide from the world. It is not a pleasant place to be and is usually experienced as a place of guilt and, even worse, shame. With guilt, there is an embarrassment for what you might or might not have done. With shame, there is an experience of humiliation for who you are. It is a soul deep experience of exposure for not being who you think you should be or for being who you believe you shouldn't be. The pain here is of experiencing this humiliating exposure and being found out for how bad you believe you really are. As a victim, people are faced with a litany of "victimizations and wrongs" that have been perpetrated on them. They launch a hidden passive aggressive attack on the individual they believe did them wrong. The difference between a victim and a martyr is that the martyr requires a witness to the wrong doing, but a victim can and often does suffer alone. The person carries within the seeds of his/her own undoing and tends to draw the very circumstance feared most. The victim always feels less than others and attempts to compensate by going into sacrifice. It could be in looking after an aging parent, or a challenged child, or always helping out each time the phone rings. Victims believe they have to do the "right thing" and have no choice.

A word of caution: These descriptions are somewhat extreme for the purposes of highlighting the underlying nature of the characteristics of this corner. In truth, we all spend some time here, and it is only a primary corner if it is our ego's predominant style (default style) of dealing with stress and threat.

Mrs. Goldfarb, Untrue Feminine, Victim & Martyr:

When I first opened my practice, one of my initial clients was a woman in her late sixties, who as it happens was there for help around sleeping. When I called her in from the waiting room, it took her close to five minutes to cover the 20 feet to my office from the waiting room. As she explained later, she had rheumatoid arthritis so badly in all her joints that she could barely move. I asked how I could help her and she began to tell me about her past, as a prelude to the presenting issue.

As it turned out, she was physically and sexually abused by her father and her eldest brother. In addition, her husband had repeatedly physically abused her, often to the point of extreme violence. As if that wasn't enough, she told me that her son had abused her and attempted to steal money from her.

My heart went out to her, and yet when I have a client that has this kind of history, it suggests that a part of her mind was complicit in these abuses. I asked her a couple of questions about why she thought these things were happening to her. She said she had no idea and that she was a regular church member and always helped out as best she could. She said that she often gave to charities, even though she didn't have the money to do so. After the many years of abuse she still had no real idea why these things were consistently happening to her…how her mind was attracting them. Sadly, she revealed that she was afraid that they were some kind of punishment and didn't want to expose her "great flaw" for fear of greater punishment.

When she finished, I said to her, "Well, I have good news and I have bad news. The good news is that I believe I can be of value to you in relation to assisting you in sleeping. What's more, I believe it will help with your rheumatoid arthritis and hopefully give you a greater range of movement and freedom. The bad news is that you may need to begin the process of letting go of your beliefs about being a victim." I could see that she was really defended against hearing the truth but I decided to be very clear and direct anyway.

She was outraged that I would even suggest that she look at her victim beliefs! Not because she found it offensive, but rather as she put it, "It is the only thing that protects me."

She wore her victim story around her like she would wear a cloak, to protect her, when what it served to do was draw the very thing to her that she was being traumatized by. I have to say that it saddened me to see her in pain and know all that she had been through and experienced. She missed seeing her role in creating the seeds of her own victimization. Fear attracts what we fear! She would have none of it. She left the office and I never saw her again. It reminded me of the choice "to be right about how others did her wrong." She had each of her scars to prove how unfairly she had been treated and did not want to have anything to do with letting that go and forgiving. But, of course, her refusal to not own the abuses and forgive them, disempowered her and allowed her to continue in the victim role, sleepless and arthritic.

I often think of her and wonder how she is managing. I hope that things have changed, but given how committed she was to her victim consciousness, it does not seem likely. I hold her in my heart and send her love nonetheless.

It is often the case that people resist exploring the role they have in creating their negative experience. That is because they hear the statement as, "It's your fault" or "You're to blame". This is not what is meant. If these negative beliefs can be reframed to "Maybe I am not completely right about..." then it opens things up for growth. What is required is to "experience" going through the middle (workshop) area of the triangles and moving toward our real truth.

Chapter 15

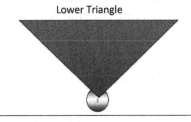

Lower Triangle

3. **Competition and Power Struggle**

Style: Anxiety-Conflict, Avoidance
Fear: Loss
Terror: Lack-Scarcity
Compensation: Indulgence
Quote: "I am right that I am not wrong!"
Ego Belief: "I must compete with others."

The ego's Competition and Power Struggle corner is marked by anxiety and conflict, all in an effort to anticipate and avoid loss. It is premised on the notion that there is not enough to go around. In a truly Darwinian sense, it is a survival of the fittest. It is all about lack and scarcity and competition. Thus, there is a perpetual state of anxiety around the loss of what the ego is most attached to.

Yet, if they are pushed and unsuccessful in their competitions they can be among the most indulgent of individuals as they attempt to compensate for their losses. They are especially in competition to avoid being stuck at one of the other two corners, with the Victim corner being the least desirable of all. They don't wish to be branded with either corner and will compete strongly to stay away from any association with either corner. They characteristically disavow any connection whatsoever with either.

A word of caution: These descriptions are somewhat extreme for the purposes of highlighting the nature and style of each corner. In truth, we all spend some time here, and it is only a primary corner if it is our ego's predominant style (default style) of dealing with stress and threat.

Becky, Competition and Power Struggle:

Becky came to counseling because of serious issues with anxiety. She had seriously debilitating anxiety and panic attacks. Yet, there was little that she would not compete around. She ran marathons and always had to be at the head of the line, whether in a grocery line or driving in traffic. She was fiercely attached to her kids and you would have thought she was competing to be mother of the month. There was little that took place that she was not part of, instilling the desire to be best in her kids as a result.

While Becky made sincere efforts to get along with everyone, invariably a conflict or power struggle would erupt, leaving her at odds with former friends. She was adept at eliminating these from her life. Because of her sociability it wasn't long before she had new friends to replace them. I could tell she was no stranger to the type of lavish lifestyle she maintained. Perhaps it was a pattern from many lifetimes, which if this was the case would take a bit more time and a different approach to transform.

When we discussed the concept of projection, Becky had real trouble with it. She said that she didn't understand it, but I always had the impression she didn't want to. When I would confront her on any of these issues she would typically deny them. In addition, she would then avoid the next few sessions, as if to say, "Don't ask those questions again." I understood her great desire for safety and the anxiety that she was continually facing.

However, as I shared with her on one occasion, her safety did not rest on her ability to compete or control, but rather on her willingness to join and partner with others; to actually extend her love and caring to others rather than set herself up as a separate and competitive force. During her counseling sessions, it would seem like she actually would get it, but then it wasn't long before she would resort to her old patterns. Old habits die hard!

She had left her husband, although she still maintained a relationship with him. While he, by comparison, was quiet, unassuming and really quite gentle, she was always very quick to point out that she had never dominated him, that it was he who had left her. Becky's approach, Corner 3, was essentially different from Corner 1 in that while she would compete, she would not be oppressive or angry in her approach.

Becky has just completed the first phase of her counseling program. I anticipate it will take a while for her to let go of the notion that she has to compete for everything. Her anxiety has improved, and the number of her actual panic attacks have diminished significantly, but she still maintains that she doesn't believe in projection. What a great gift will enter her life when she is able to embrace, not just the notion of projections, but the actual truth of this defense mechanism in her life.

Chapter 16

Middle "Workshop" Area

No problem can be resolved at the level it was created on. It is just an eternal struggle until we begin to see we need a higher order of understanding and consciousness in order to create a viable resolution. Here we are not talking about compromise. Compromise ensures no one wins and neither party truly gets what they want. True resolution needs to come from a higher order of consciousness.

This is where we need to begin to do the work. The path out of the illusions of the ego's lower triangle, leads initially through the Middle (workshop) Area. As we follow the arrow from our primary corner, we must pass through three steps to free ourselves from our ego corner. This asks that we:

1. **Own our projections (cognitive):** Whatever beliefs and judgments we hold actually arise from our own subconscious mind and "un-owned potentialities." These are often so unacceptable to our conscious mind that we have needed to stuff them in our subconscious to avoid having to address them. They are forced to surface outside of ourselves in the form of a projection on the "reality" objects of our concern in order for us to deal with them.

2. **Forgive all (emotional):** If we have accused, judged others because of the things we have projected onto them, then all needs to be forgiven, especially the objects of our projections and our self. Forgiveness is firstly the cancelling of all indictments against the objects of our attack (including ourselves). Secondly, it is the release of any and all emotional resentment and bitterness associated with these targets. Thirdly, it is the giving forth of all the love withheld while we were busy being right. Fourthly, fore-give in advance, in the event that what triggered us happens again.

3. **Surrender (physical):** This is **letting it all go** and **letting it be - as it is!** It is not wishing things were different, trying to make them different, or withdrawing because there must be something wrong. It is the true acceptance of who we are, what we are, where we are, why we are, because we have chosen to offer **no resistance to what is - as it is.**

1. Own Your Projections:

This has been a difficult concept for some people to grasp, and yet it is one of the primary principles of the mind. What we perceive within ourselves, both positive and negative, and we cannot claim either because we judge ourselves unworthy, or we cannot accept due to our shame, we are unconsciously bound to project outwards. What we project outwards and deny, is intended to reinforce our perception of our own primary limits. Used negatively, it is a form of reinforcing other people's guilt, judging it, and thereby proclaiming its absence in ourselves. It is an attempt to shift responsibility for something by placing it on someone else, even though it originates in our own mind.

I will give a "brief account" of what I consider a classic case of owning your projections that occurred recently with a client, named Jarred, who was in counseling, requested by his employer, due to his poor relations with his fellow employees. He was in the habit of referring to other guys he worked with as "gay", in a belittling and demeaning voice and manner. I had seen him for several sessions during which time we discussed the issue in question. He generally dismissed the matter saying that there were "just some hurt feelings" and there was nothing more to it. He even joked in the session about how the "faggots were taking over the office."

I reminded him that "that was precisely what had gotten him into trouble and could be considered harassment." He was silent for a period of time during which I could see he was processing what had just taken place. I had observed that he likely was on the victim martyr corner, and after several sessions, I asked him if he felt safe in my office, to which he replied, "Yes, I do," then paused.

"Do you mind if I ask you what you were just reflecting on?"

He quickly flushed and seemed embarrassed.

He said, "Well I think I may have those tendencies, but I am not sure."

"Would it be OK if you were?" I asked.

"Sort of...here anyway," he answered. "But I would give anything to not be or change it."

I replied, "Well, I am not sure that's anything we could or should do here, but would you settle for accepting yourself more fully as you are?"

"Yes," he smiled. He was slowly beginning to accept his projections.

2. Forgive All:

I continued to see Jarred over a period of weeks but things were moving slowly as we would hit places of resistance where he would rebel against accepting this aspect of himself. He was making progress overall and had pretty much stopped his demeaning interactions at work. When I asked him how he felt at work, he shrugged his shoulders and said, "OK, I guess". "Is there something we should discuss in relation to your interactions at work?" "No, not really. It's just that I have behaved that way for so long it's hard to stop the old ways of behaving, and when I am out with friends, I still make those comments."

"Nobody at work or among my friends knows about me." I asked, "How do you feel about yourself when you still make those comments?" "I feel terrible about myself, just terrible like...,"he paused. "Like...?" I encouraged, waiting for his response. But he could not or would not complete his sentence.

It continued like that for the next couple of sessions and I was not wanting to crowd him. I finally asked what it was that he had stopped short of saying, and reminded him of the statement he was in the process of making just before he stopped. "I feel terrible about myself, just terrible. I felt like I did when I was a teenager and my father would tease me and humiliate me about being a 'Nancy boy.' I wanted his respect but all I got was his ridicule. I hate him for that! I feel such shame, such toxic shame."

I had him picture his father on a chair in front of him and asked him what he would like to say to him. He flushed with anger and said, "I hate you for doing what you did to me. All I wanted was your love and respect and you just embarrassed and humiliated me. I hate you for that." I asked what was happening with his father as he shared that with him. "He is just sneering at me," replied Jarred. "Are you basing that on what you are seeing in his face in your image of him, or is that just how you think he would respond?" There was silence for a bit as he considered the matter, then he began to cry. He said that when he looked in his father's eyes there was sadness and tears. I asked him what he was feeling and he said he felt sorry for him. "Are you willing to forgive him?" I asked. "No, not yet," he said, "maybe later." I suggested he write to his father and share his anger and his forgiveness with him by letter.

3. Acceptance and Surrender:

Jarred told me he never actually did write the letter to his father. I asked him why, and he said he just could not bring himself to do it, and the more time that passed, the less inclined he was to do it. "You know the forgiveness is really more for you than it is for your father," I commented. Jarred just shrugged and went a bit limp.

I really care for Jarred and would like to be able to report that he made a complete breakthrough and stepped into full acceptance of himself and his father. However, he ran into resistance here and found he was unable to move forward on his path. His employer ceased funding his sessions and Jarred decided he would take a break from the counseling.

Acceptance of our clients and their challenges is one of the key aspects of all counseling; patience is as well. Ultimately, the ability to surrender to the true nature of what is happening, both in and out of the session, is a true sign of a growing spiritual humility.

For me, it was particularly difficult to accept that a client (Jarred) could be so close to a point of full acceptance and yet not take the step forward. I do not have the full picture though and I will need to take a closer look at what it is in me that would have been so caught up in Jarred's progress.

My ability to accept and surrender completely to the overall reality, "**exactly as it is**", is still a bit of a stretch at times. And yet, so much is dependent on my level of consciousness, the openness of my heart, and the level of willingness I find myself in at any point in time.

I suppose I can always accept my own limits, much as I would my client's. And if I am struggling with that level of acceptance I can always accept that I am struggling to accept my "limitations of acceptance". Part of my challenge, I believe, has to do with feeling so close to a transformational shift that I have difficulty accepting anything other than that specific higher outcome. Thank you, Jarred!

Transition To A Higher Calling:

The **Upper Triangle** then comes into play once we have completed all three of the steps in the middle area. Notice the arrows. The corner where the arrow has ended is the upper corner we are being called to, but where we are still refusing to go. We prefer to stay hidden rather than respond to and honor our higher calling, our higher state of being, and our Greatness.

We are afraid to take up and model the Leadership, Empowerment, and Vision we were called to model and share with others. In the **Leadership and Purpose corner,** we are being asked to come out of hiding, to show the way to others, especially those we love. To the degree we are unwilling to give this gift to the world, through our willing Presence, we are forced by our ego back into the lower triangle, or to remain in the ego fear based victim and martyr role. This is a special case of "specialness" (see Glossary) and is very painful, of course, because of the lengths we need to go to, to be special. **It is painful to be small, when you are called to be Great.**

This is true as well for the **Empowerment and Love corner.** Here we are being asked to share our gift of Love, unconditionally, and to use this gift to step towards our partners, and to support and facilitate their unconditional empowerment. This is difficult because the corner we are coming from is the arrogance and oppression corner. The ego's fear would, of course, taunt us with the fear of a loss of being, of being nothing at all. It is difficult to embrace Love (the true equalizer) and to serve by empowering others (when they may see themselves as better than us), especially when we are and have been so attached to "specialness". It is hard to give so much (anonymously) and yet not be recognized, or seen as a heroic being.

The **Cooperation, Partnership and Vision corner** is an invitation to join with others in the Co-creative Manifestation of a Sacred and Shared Vision. This is ultimately joining in the Intimate Communion of all beings in Love, and manifesting this creation in the form of a Heaven on earth. However, past experiences of feeling that it has always been necessary to be in competition and power struggle, in order to survive and to be special, make it a difficult step to take, due to the perceived lack and scarcity. It's hard to join with others, and share, when they may take what you believe is yours alone.

Chapter 17

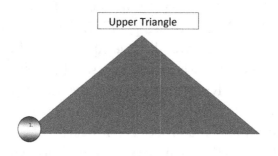

Upper Triangle

1.Leadership and Purpose

True Masculine

Key: Courage

Soul Qualities: Clarity, Focus, Strength

Quote: We guide you in Love.

The upper triangle #1 corner is Leadership and Purpose. Who would have guessed that a former victim/martyr could transform into a spiritual leader and extender of spiritual purpose. Take heart, all of you, who would find yourself mired in lower triangle #2, the ego's victim/martyr corner. Ask yourself, "Am I in hiding? Is there a higher calling I am ignoring?" If the answer is "yes" or "maybe," then you may well be a candidate for the upper triangle #1 corner. The good news is that you are not alone. Even a little willingness can go a long way toward inviting the guidance and support you need. The bad news is that you may need to let go of a lot of your victim story and that may be all you have ever known about yourself (though never true about you anyway). Remember Mrs. Goldfarb, who had become so attached to her victim story that she wasn't willing to let go of it? The key quality of the upper triangle and the #1 corner is the capacity for enormous courage, love and leadership. It is the highest calling of the Victim/Martyr corner. It taps into the highest qualities of the soul which come as you "ask for help." I know you may have asked and prayed dozens of times. Just try it with a tiny bit of willingness to move forward; even a microscopic amount will begin the process. I mean, you are reading this book, right? Do you think that happened by chance? Not a chance! It is you who must take the first step. It is no accident you are holding the key to your future greatness in your hands. Ask for help and let your life be "as if" it has always been that way. This is truly a very powerful heuristic to try out.

I watched a documentary on student depression/suicide and it was very disturbing to see that it is the second leading cause of death amongst students (with auto accidents first). One of the people being interviewed, a young girl named Erin Hodgson, had lived for half her life fighting the stigma of depression. Even at age twelve she was devastated at hearing the negative comments that were being said about her. Her sense of worthlessness and rejection was overwhelming, because nobody wanted to be friends with her, or even in her presence. She was crushed by her experiences and thought of herself as a weird, worthless loser.

Her first thought of suicide came at an early age, as a child, when she asked her parents to "have her put down." It plagued her all along the way. She went to live in residence at the University of Toronto. Her depression deepened and darkened while she lived in residence. There, she attempted suicide and almost succeeded. After recovering from her attempt, her fellow residents were asked if they wanted her back. They took a vote and asked her to leave. To Erin, this was the consummate statement of rejection because of her worthlessness.

Over time and with help, Erin overcame her challenges. In the spring of 2013, she graduated from Toronto's Humber College. When asked why she was willing to speak publicly and on camera and why she didn't "just try to hide it," since it could come back on her in terms of employment, she said, "Somebody needs to talk about it and if I don't then who will?" She is now one of a group of students leading the way in generating increased awareness of student mental health issues and ending the stigmas. Erin is a co-leader for www.thejackproject.org

2. Personal and Transpersonal Empowerment Triangles

Copyright 1990© James F. Shea & The Institute for Transpersonal Empowerment

Transpersonal Levels of Higher Consciousness

Key: *Inspiration*
Soul Qualities: *Openness, Acceptance, Joining*
"We join with you in Love."
Cooperation and Vision

Essence-Spirit
GREATNESS
Love and
Partnership
(Inspiration Guided)

Key: *Courage*
Soul Qualities: *Clarity, Focus, Strength*
"We guide you in Love."
Leadership and Purpose

Key: *Compassion*
Soul Qualities: *Grace, Support, Love*
""'We step toward you in Love.'"'
Empowerment and Love

Physical	3. Acceptance and Surrender.	
Emotional	2. Openness and Forgiveness.	
Mental	1. Willingness to Own Projections.	

TRANSFORMATIONAL BRIDGE

EMPOWERMENT PROCESSING

Ego-Illusion
SPECIALNESS
Fear and
Separation
(Adrenalin driven)

Arrogance and Oppression

Style: *Anger, Attack, Denial,*
Fear: *Anonymity.*
Terror: *Nothingness, Non-Being.*
Compensation: *Tantrum,*
Quote: *"I am right (that I am right)."*
Core Belief: *I am better than others!*

Victim and Martyr

Style: *Depression, Withdrawal, Hiding.*
Fear: *Exposure.*
Terror: *Guilt and Shame*
Compensation: *Sacrifice.*
Quote: *I am right, (that you are wrong.)*
Core Belief: *I am worse than others!*

Competition and Power Struggle
Style: *Anxiety-Conflict, Avoidance*
Fear: *Loss.*
Terror: *Lack-Scarcity.*
Compensation: *Indulgence.*
Quote: *"I am right (that I am not wrong)."*
Core Belief: *I must compete to survive!*

Personal Levels of Ego Consciousness

Chapter 18

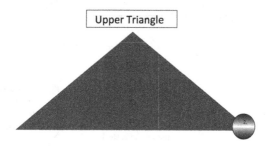

Upper Triangle

2.**Empowerment and Love**

True Feminine

Key: Compassion

Soul Qualities: Grace, Support, Ease

Quote: We step toward you in Love.

The Upper Triangle #**2.Empowerment and Love** corner, is where we are being called to share our gift of Love, unconditionally, and to use this gift to step towards our partners to support and facilitate their unconditional empowerment. The soul qualities are Grace, Support, and Ease. Those with this calling share these gifts generously for the benefit of mankind. The key to this corner is a deep level of compassion for the human condition. At this level, we are joined, both inside and out, by transpersonally oriented individuals who share a similar vision of love and are willing to be part of a sacred sharing. Rarely will these individuals be new to each other, having worked together before to bring grace to a people who are faltering. The beneficial outcome of their contribution is to reduce and shorten the time and pain needed by others to find the light in the midst of their darkness.

The difficulty here is in the transition to a corner requiring such a high level of humility. Remember, the ego corner we are coming from is the arrogance or oppression corner. The ego's fear would, of course, taunt us with a loss of being, of being nothing at all, which is a true statement about the actual status of the ego.

It is difficult to embrace Love, which is the true equalizer, and to serve by empowering others, when they may see themselves as better than us, especially when we are and have been so attached to specialness. It is hard to give so much and still be anonymous and not be recognized or seen as a heroic being.

I keep thinking about Paul the Apostle (Saul) and his marvelous transformation from his oppressive persecution of Christians to becoming one of the most empowering of all Christian apostles. While on his way to Damascus to continue his attack on Christian converts, he was transformed following a vision of Christ. He went on to become one of the greatest of the Christian apostles, spreading the message of Christ's Love and Christianity near and far.

Paul said of Christ, that He was the One "through whom we have received Grace...including you who are called." I believe it may have been former President Jimmy Carter who said, "Love is not passive, it is active. If people build walls to keep love out, then surround those walls with love. Love is real, but the walls are not."

Chapter 19

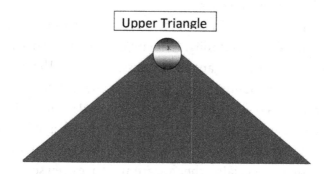

3.Cooperation, Partnership and Vision

Key: Inspiration

Soul Qualities: Openness, Joining

Quote: We join you in Love.

In the Upper Triangle, the **Cooperation, Partnership, Vision corner** is at the apex of the triangle. It embodies the totality of all that has gone before and is the synthesis of all that is true in both masculine and feminine principles. It is the ultimate joining and partnership of both principles in the Sacred Marriage of the ultimate vision of co-creation.

It is creating Heaven on Earth as an experience for all humanity to share and be part of. The key here is the Presence of Spirit infusing and inspiring all of humanity, as the Soul awakens in each, and the capacity for true cooperation, partnership and joining is finally manifest on earth. Is this a dream?

No, it is a vision! A vision for humanity rooted deeply in our human hearts. It is a shared vision of hope and love for all of humanity. It is our highest aspiration as human beings, to join with all others in a union so profound and so persistent that no amount of darkness can extinguish it.

The **Cooperation, Partnership and Vision corner** is an invitation to join with all others in the Co-creative Manifestation of a Sacred and Shared Vision. This is ultimately joining in the intimate communion of all beings in love, and manifesting this creation in the form of a Heaven on earth. However, past experiences of feeling that it has always been necessary to be in competition and power struggle, in order to survive and to be special, make it a difficult step to take due to the perceived lack and scarcity. It is hard to join with others, and share, when they may take what you believe is yours.

A classic example of this is when former rivals join together to support each other against a larger threat. When Olympic teams are created, they are often made up of former competitors and rivals. Sometimes this competition can be quite fierce. However, you can see this marvelous and miraculous transformation take place as they become part of the same vision and begin to subjugate their egos. For each member of a team, for example an Olympic hockey team, each individual may well be the top all round player on his home team. He may in fact be the star on the team.

And yet all this fame and stardom needs to be set aside, to join with others facing the same challenge. This cannot happen if the conflict and competition isn't released. "Leave your ego at the door!" is the statement that is used over and over. In a team sport, at that level, true partnership is required or the team doesn't gel. True cooperation is the baseline for success in Olympic hockey. The teams that achieve the most are not always the teams with the greatest talent and ability; they are the ones that have taken their full talent to the next level, guided by a vision of success.

This is the same for all human endeavors. People would need to not only see and feel a higher vision for that endeavor, they would need to be willing to begin to live it "as if true" already.

Chapter 20

Relationship Empowerment Triangles

The Personal & Transpersonal Levels

I believe a brief summary may be in order just to make sure we are on the same page.

The Upper and Lower Empowerment Triangles are heuristic devices designed to reflect both the personal ego and transpersonal spirit levels of our consciousness. They are both very precise in identifying where the primary roadblock to spiritual growth is located, why, and at the same time offering the direction out of blockage and towards true spiritual growth.

They are, in fact, a road map to assist us in locating where we are in the process of rising above the limits of our beliefs and in identifying the nature of the fear that holds it all in place. For example, each corner of the lower triangle carries one of three conditions of the ego, what holds that condition in place, and the non-productive ways we've developed for coping with this state.

The Lower triangle represents the 3 personal corner points of ego and the lower levels of consciousness. Since almost all of us are stuck in some form of limiting ego consciousness, it is safe to assume that we can be located somewhere on the three corners of the lower triangle. It is easy to see where we are emotionally located in any relationship and observe how this can change as we examine our position in relation to others, including our own soul.

The Upper triangle represents the three transpersonal points and the higher levels of consciousness where our consciousness is guided by the qualities of our soul, filled with Spirit. We do not go alone at these levels. Rather, we are working co-creatively towards a shared vision of love on earth.

In the highest triangle, we are supported both from within and without as we begin to flow in our lives. Each transpersonal point is in alignment with that of our soul, and we find support at each point to assist us in the co-creative process of manifesting heaven on earth.

The real secret of happiness is in following your true purpose, aligned with your soul and Spirit. Nothing could make anyone happier. The challenge of achieving this level of consciousness depends on our ability to rise above the ego, which in turn begins with our willingness, however small.

The first step towards this rise in consciousness is to locate where you are in the lower triangle. Clearly examine all the issues associated with that point-of-view and then begin the process of heuristically checking out the 3-steps in the middle Workshop Area between the lower and upper triangles. The middle area, which if the arrow is followed, is capable of lifting us out of the ego's limited beliefs, perceptions, emotions and fear based structures. This move will take us from what is untrue to what is true, from beliefs to knowing, from the fear based illusions of the ego to the ultimate truth of our soul and Spirit.

The middle area is the present "here and now" moment, our true and only point of power and choice. I call the middle area the workshop area because, to those willing to work these steps, we begin to heal our life, our relationships and our soul. But, it requires work. For many, it can seem as though this is never going to end. Yet, it is important to remember we cannot move forward until we are dealing in the truth of reality rather than the ego's illusions.

Without question, the workshop middle area is the area that we are all needing to most work. It is said that forgiveness is love on the earthly plane, so what else could we be doing that would be a better thing to do with our time and space?

LEVELS OF TRANSPERSONAL EMPOWERMENT

1. **Highest Levels** of Consciousness - Sacred Intimacy, Communion:
   There is only Love (and it has no opposite).
   There is only Here.
   There is only Now.

THEME: Living in Grace (Divine Levels)
(Levels of Mastery; Co-Creativity; Sacred Choice; Sacred Purpose; Sacred Love; Heaven on earth; Living Love)

LEVELS OF PERSONAL EMPOWERMENT

2. **Working Levels** of Consciousness: Releasing Limits on Love:

   There is only Forgiveness
   There are no Accidents
   There are only Mirrors

THEME: Decoding of Life Experiences (Workshop Levels)
(Levels of Clearing perception; Karma burning; Accountability in Creation; Understanding Cause-Effect; Releasing withdrawal and withhold on Love; Willing to choose; Taking responsibility)

LEVELS OF PERSONAL DISEMPOWERMENT

3. **Lowest Levels** of Consciousness: Illusion, Blockage, Pain:

   There is only Fear, Loneliness and Separation.
   There is only Shame, Pain, Addictive-Compulsions.
   There are only Accidents, Shock, Denial and Death.

THEME: Blind and Rebellious; Kicking & Screaming (Pain)
(Levels of Hiding and Denial; Giving up our "Power to Choose"; Disempowered Creation (Karma); Power Struggle; Withdrawing and Withhold Love; Holding on, Being Right; Blame:No Accountability)

LEVELS OF CONSCIOUSLY EMPOWERED LIVING - LOVING

Chapter 21

Transpersonal Empowerment

"We are One with the Source of all Creation!
All is Communion; All is Intimacy"

The previous relationship Heuristics serve as a visual map to the basic three levels of Potential Consciousness Experience in any relationship. While they are intended to be self-explanatory, perhaps a bit of clarification wouldn't hurt.

Most of humanity functions somewhere between Level 2 and Level 3. Level 3 is the most painful level of conscious experience because we are as yet still unaware of levels of objective reality, and we live within limiting belief systems in a world of illusions. Here we would rather be right than true. It is, at its deepest and darkest core, an experience of Hell. "I would rather rule in Hell than just be a drop in the ocean of Heaven" (See Lower Triangle-Arrogance). At these deeper levels of extreme illusion and pain, it is very easy to succumb to drugs and alcohol, even passive suicide and suicidal panic can become a preferred reality for many...too many!

Thus, at these levels, regret is a Gift because it can initiate a process of **"willingness to not be right"**. This is not to say that you were wrong; it's simply that you acknowledge **"maybe**

I was just not right". It is at this point of willingness that our consciousness can exercise choice again. Even a small and imperfect willingness is a place to begin and it has enormous value in moving us forward. We just need to keep moving, taking the next step forward until we get to Level 2, where we begin to discover how our life experiences have brought us to a new level.

If in spite of gentle, almost imperceptible nudges from the soul (in the beginning), to the very extremes of **shocks, accidents and death,** there still has been no movement by the ego, nor even any willingness to do so, the soul may begin to slowly withdraw its essence in favor of offering another life opportunity to the individual's "Call of the Soul".

Once the ego has begun to grow in willingness and openness to truly "seeing", our progress begins to move more quickly. We begin to explore Level 2 (There are no accidents, only our mirrors), somewhat briefly at first, but then as the reality of its truth actually expresses in our lives, we choose to live in this "workshop" consciousness more and more. At Level 2, we are somewhat free of Level 3, but we are still prone to being drawn back into the lower levels. It is clear, however, that it will never completely ensnare and enslave our will and freedom to choose ever again.

At Level 2 we begin to see our life as more purposeful. We begin to slowly unravel the mystery of our life experiences and the many so called "accidents", as well as our projections. We begin to decode the hieroglyphics of meaning encoded in our experience. There are, of course, many levels within Level 2, and it can seem like it is taking forever to make any lasting progress. Relationships offer a great gift to us at this level.

In addition, gifts like living the Ho'oponopono prayer can accelerate our progress greatly (see Appendix for a more extensive list of resources). There are increasingly more empowerment workshops and seminars, books, counselors and guides. They all share certain commonalities with the middle section of the empowerment triangles. These commonalities are: owning your projections, forgiveness, and willingness to respond to the Call to Greatness.

Moving to Level 1 is at present a multiple lifetime project for most of us. I know in my own lives I have held this Vision of Love for a very long time. Typically, I manage to get a portion of it but have rarely been able to put it all together.

There have been times when I have enjoyed the reality of a Higher Love, and lived in a moment of truth. I suspect many have, more than we realize. However, my experience, over lifetimes, is that I find myself often experiencing a fall from Grace. It is usually a place where I have become frightened, for whatever reason, and then put the brakes on. Like the recent experience where I wandered into a three to four month sink hole, before rising again.

From where my consciousness is at this moment as I write, it seems unbelievable to me that I could have gotten stuck at such a low level for so long, and yet it happens. As I have reviewed my most recent lives, I see that I much more preferred to receive than to give, not so much in a material sense as in a spiritual one. I had the habit of accumulating wisdom, knowledge and experience but refused to publicly share what I had gathered, for fear of being made to pay dearly for my "gift sharing". In fact, I have recollections of dying painfully, accused of being a heretic. So guess what surfaces in relation to writing this book?

"You got it...my fear of taking that next step and sharing my gift", as in writing this book. In those lifetimes, I always thought that God would arrive and "slay" those who were busy slaying me. Never happened, that I can recall, so why am I here again? Well, to give the "gift of sharing" that I have been so unsuccessful at fully giving previously. Contrary to my earlier proclamation of being finished while in my previous slump, my work here is not yet done.

So, my strategies of staying very close to the wall and not being the highest nail, (you know, the one that gets hammered first), have not really worked. I want to hang out in Level 1, but keep running into spooky things that need to be addressed first.

Level 1 is an experiential place of Knowing, Grace and Love. It is filled with Grace, Ease and Vision. I could not write this little book from any place other than Level 1. It is filled with Flow, Inspiration, and a capacity to create Clarity and Direction. It is for others, at least as much as it is for me.

If I look back at the triangles, I can see that historically, I have held a victim/martyr consciousness and have been reluctant to take up my leadership role, blaming God (of course) for not being there for me. The reason I was unable to write this before, was that I was not at a level of consciousness that held sufficient energy to manifest the expression of Love that is needed to give this gift. I was vibrating at the level of fear, Level 3, at that time. Not much worthwhile comes out of that level except our consciousness when we are ready.

Can I continue to move forward and when I get stalled, try "as if" being in Level 1? I sure hope so. I am a "Grace and Ease addict," what some might call lazy. I say, "Nay, nay," as comedian John Pinette was fond of saying. Regardless though, what I do know about this level is I am not alone here. I am joined by others. In fact, what I love the most is the quality of intimacy and communion I feel here with other beings of light, both in and out of form. Also, I know the way home, as well as how to get myself and others there. I invite you all to join me, if it works for you.

Chapter 22

Relationship As A Spiritual Path

"Our relationships will tend to mirror the nature of our projections, and the conspiracy against our Greatness. Transformed, our relationships become one of the greatest gifts, especially as they lead us to our Presence and who we really are."

There are correspondences between the Relationship Triangles, the Levels of Consciously Empowered Loving, and of course the Stages of Relationship. So, you may ask, why is the focus of this book on healing our conspiracy, all about our relationships?

Relationships are one of the key elements in the healing of our ego conspiracy. They are the mirror that reflects each of our own ego blockages and they are reflected in the 3 corners of the Lower Triangle, the lowest levels of the Levels of Love Heuristics (Levels 1-3), and the early stages of relationship.

Our relationships tend to play out in ways that reflect our ego conspiracy. During the first three stages of relationship we project our ego issues onto our partner. There is no real relationship here.

However, if we are able to decode the dynamics of our relationships and own our projections, then we stand a very good chance of transforming our ego blocks and moving on to our Greatness – who we really are. The Relationship Heuristic (Level 2), once practiced, is particularly useful in this decoding process.

This is also true with the triangles. As we get more feedback on the issues the ego is running, we get to see the direction of growth and the eventual path to Greatness. The key here is the nature of each ego corner, what the ego's fear is, what the ego's core belief is, how the ego attempts to express itself, compensate for its condition, and what terrorizes it.

There are three underlying issues that clients come to counseling for. These issues are anger, anxiety and depression. These are underlying conditions, and the client is usually unaware of the hidden emotional condition. This surfaces as smoking, lack of confidence, sickness, insomnia, relationship issues, etc. They are only consciously aware of their presenting issue, but underneath lies an emotional center that holds the core in place.

Thus, a key part of addressing the conspiracy of the ego is to dismantle the emotional and psychic core of the issue, located on your primary corner on the triangle. I say primary because we are capable of being polarized under the right circumstances on any of the other two corners. For example, maybe we find ourselves on the victim/martyr corner and as a rule embodying the elements of that corner. However, if someone deliberately tries to hurt us, we may find ourselves leaping into the attack mode. But, under normal circumstances, we tend to gravitate to our primary corner, as the default, and therein lies the core of our ego blockage.

If we examine the stages of relationship, we can see that real relationship only begins at the fourth stage, as we begin to take responsibility and become more accountable for all that we experience, regardless of its origin. This begins the ego decoding process which eventually will set us free. In this way, we no longer need our partner to be a particular way so that we can feel better about ourselves. Relationships at this level tend to be much more stable and tend to last, or last longer than those that are dramatically structured around the romance and intensity of the first stage, which is a projection of our fantasy of Mr./Mrs. Right. We cannot move on with our growth and development until we have addressed the issue of our projections and yet they are often difficult to see much less address. Thus, with the help of the Relationship Triangles, the distinct Levels of Consciously Empowered Loving, and the Stages of Relationship, it is easier to spot these projections using these tools as maps or charts of the psychological terrain. In fact they also serve as a guide to where we actually are in the development of our consciousness, and what might be standing in our way.

The Relationship Triangles quite simply identify not only how our ego likes to position itself in a relationship, but also reveal what the underlying ego dynamics are, that need to be addressed in order to move forward spiritually. So, in a very simple way, these charts help "kill two birds with one stone", and at the same time point to the way out... the way beyond.

When these are combined with the Heuristic Devices, we have a very simple and yet very powerful approach to accelerating our own relationships, and our spiritual progress. These are the Simple Gifts we have all been given to move us forward to abundance, liberation and enlightenment.

Chapter 23

A Vision of Greatness

Our Greatness is ultimately the single highest achievement as a human being. It is the culmination of lifetimes of effort and growth. It is the Omega point of our individual development and growth. It is the point from which we become whole and complete.

In each of us is the potential for Greatness. Our deepest and most valued gifts, talents, abilities, strengths often remain hidden even from ourselves. At a deeper level still lie our Purpose, Vision and the Essence of who we are most truly. It is what the eminent psychologist Dr. A.H. Maslow described as "one's own Greatness" and is hidden because of our ego's fear.

Truly understood in the light of Peak Psychology and the contents of this book, we see we have been engaged in a fear based conspiracy to cover and block our own highest expression and our greatest gift to humanity. There is at once a desire to know and a fear of knowing.

To feel our permission and authority to be **"wholly who we are"** is both our empowerment and our transpersonal empowerment.

Our Greatness is our willingness to express that empowerment through our freedom and liberation. It is the ultimate expression of our Creativity, Spontaneity and Innocence. It is our gift of Grace to a world enslaved in ignorance of its True Being. When we choose to give the gift of our service in Love, to truly contribute to the lives of others in a joyous way, then we begin to touch our own Greatness.

It is the highest contribution we can make on this planet, to use our love as the light which supports, empowers and guides us out of the imprisonment of our ego into the light of our Greatness. However, before we can do this, a **transformation** of the identity formerly known as the ego needs to take place. This is the process of letting go of who we perceived ourselves to be. This is the journey of Emergence to Greatness, to who we really are.

The old ways continue to call us back and try to hold us back. But our willingness, openness and acceptance of what is calling us forth is a much more powerful pull. Only one principle is necessary, and it does not require perfection. As A Course in Miracles points out, it requires only a "little willingness" to choose. You are not called upon to do what one "still divided against oneself," would find impossible. "Have a little faith" that wisdom and grace will find you, even in spite of your state of mind. This is the promise that awaits you...and the promise of your Greatness.

Chapter 24

The Final Chapter

What if all who could see this higher vision were fully willing to live it now, today, at this very moment? To dare to walk out into the world as if the vision was fully and globally manifesting. What do you think would happen? What if everyone began to share the vision in a spirit of love?

In the pursuit of a global shift in consciousness, it would be necessary for all of us to see the same or very similar vision for humanity. That's tough to do while you are starving, or dying of thirst, or engaged in international conflicts and competition for financial and political success. Just to end world poverty, hunger, and disease would require an enormous shift in consciousness.

And yet, in spite all that would stand between us, a critical mass is actually achieved that sweeps up all those who desire to be set free. This is the highest attainment of a willing humanity, carried on the shoulders of all who have labored long in the gardens of the Spirit. In one sense, it is the realization of humanity's deepest, most innocent and most abiding vision.

It is a communion of intimacy wherein all souls return home, together as one.

We were as one...
And yet not Whole.
We divided for the sake of Love,
In the hope of Communion,
Wholly, as one.
Infinitely, Eternally,
Universally One.

This flame still lives within each of us, an innocent and a guiding light...a hope, a dream and a Vision that this time, will take us all the way home.

APPENDICES

Appendix A

Heuristic Exercise (As if true): To be completed following 3-6 weeks

Print out several copies of this Heuristic Exercise for your personal use in exploring the Heuristic Statement in this chapter as well as in chapters throughout this book.

Write the Heuristic idea to be explored over the next few weeks:

Following your exploration of your "as if true" statement, write your answer to the following questions* in a Journal. Be as complete as you can in your answers.

1) Does the statement seem true or untrue? Why?
2) Can the statement be seen as both true and untrue? Why?
3) Do you have an emotional or any reaction to the statement?
4) How does it affect your life to see it that way?
5) Why do you think you view the statement the way you do?
6) Do you feel more freedom? Empowered? Confident? Why?

7) How would Buddha? Christ? family and friends? answer the above questions in light of the statement being explored. Take one point-of-view at a time.

*Typically heuristics would be self-generated and these questions are simply guidelines. Please feel free to write in your own questions.

Useful Heuristic Affirmations

We are one with the source of all creation!
All is as it should be!
In Truth, nothing is wrong!
We are co-creators in the Universe!
We are all connected through Spirit!
Nothing real can be threatened!
Nothing unreal exists!
Herein lies the peace of God!
Limits are beliefs to be transcended!
In the province of the mind, there are no limits!
I embrace all that supports my well-being!
Change my mind, change my life!
It is my destiny to be Great!
I always claim my projections!
I forgive all and move forward in my life!
As I give my light, darkness disappears!
There is only Love, and it has no opposite!
There is only Here and Now!
There are no accidents, I decode this experience!
There are only mirrors!
There is only forgiveness!

Glossary

Accountability: Taking full responsibility for our creations and our lives. No Blame.

Affirmation: A statement of that which we hope to bring about in our life, by continuously affirming. See Heuristic Affirmations.

Belief: What we speculate is true, but do not know is true.

Co-creativity: A stage of relationship where we work in harmony cooperatively with our partner, and others.

Conspiracy: A hidden, surreptitious, plot formulated by the ego, in secret, and formulated against the truth of our Greatness.

Construct: Not having real existence independent of the mind(s) of the observer(s).

Communion: To connect/share so deeply and intimately that nothing stands between you and what you are in communion with.

Disempowerment: That which does not value, support or nurture our True nature.

Ego: A construct that purports that illusions are real and that it is real.

Empowerment: That condition which authorizes, gives permission and support for who we are, and our True nature.

Energy: Communicating the idea of flow, movement, vibration. Not as in physics, but as in a form of connection with others.

Fear (two types): Basic hardwired fear which supports physical survival; psychic fear which is the ego's illusion of reality.

Forgiving: Cancelling all judgments, indictments, releasing our withhold on love, and giving ourselves back to life.

Gift: What we choose to give unconditionally to others because we care about them.

Grace: A gift that reduces and/or eliminates the amount of pain and suffering, or the amount of time needed to move forward.

Greatness: Our true state of Being. Our true nature. Who we really are beyond our ego's illusions.

Heuristic: Methods of "as if" discovery that encourage learners to discover solutions for themselves. Not rigid or rule bound.

Heuristic Affirmation: Using applied heuristics as a way of exploring, discovering, affirming the value of a belief for us.

Heuristic Device: Any of a number of devices to assist in the Heuristic process ex. charts, graphs, graphics.

Heuristic Exploration: The process of living "as if true" in an effort to determine a statement's value to us. Checking it out.

Higher Being: Referencing a higher level of consciousness we are experiencing, or that someone else is experiencing.

Illusions: Aspects of our mind and perception that attribute a level of reality to what is not real.

Intimacy: A state or process of removing all blocks that would stand in the way of true communion. A place of no barriers.

Knowing: A one to one relationship with what is. No mediation by perception or belief.

Presence: That Authentic Being which we are most truly and deeply. Being present in the now moment.

Projections: Unowned judgments that exist in our subconscious mind, that we externalize onto others, to hide our own guilt.

Psychic: A level of our feeling experience subject to illusions, and distortions. Does not refer to forms of intuitive knowing.

Sacred: To be, or to make eternal. Principles of True Love or Loving. Timeless truth, eternal realities and guidelines.

Separation: The illusion that we are separate from our source. What we choose to try and create in our world.

Soul: That level of our higher mind that is eternal and offers guidance and assistance. A bridge to Spirit.

Specialness: Ego's attempt to compensate for not living our True Purpose. Attempting to do things "our way" as a compensation for not doing things "God's way" and daring to be Great. A "saccharin substitute" for our Greatness.

Spirit: That aspect of our source which offers our soul guidance and support.

Surrender: Allowing the love which is within to surface for expression and extension, and receiving love from everywhere.

Transpersonal: Moving beyond the purely personal in our life to assist, serve and support others.

Transpersonal Empowerment: Giving ourselves full permission to be wholly who we are in the service and support of humanity.

Truth: That which exists beyond belief and conjecture. The nature of our knowing as beings of greatness.

Untrue Feminine: That which presents itself as of the feminine principle but in actuality is an illusion mired in ego.

Untrue masculine: That which presents itself as of the masculine principle but in actuality is an illusion mired in ego.

For Links to additional Resources, see "Resources" page online.

For ideas on setting up or managing groups, see "Groups" page online.

http://www.quantumempowermentinstitute.com
http://www.quantumempowerment.com

Appendix B

Simple Gifts

'Tis the gift to be simple, 'tis the gift to be free,

'Tis the gift to come down where you ought to Be,

And when we find ourselves in the place just right,

'Twill be in the valley of love and delight.

When true simplicity is gain'd,

To bow and to bend we shan't be asham'd,

To turn, turn will be our delight,

Till by turning, turning we come round right.

Old Shaker Song, Elder J. Bracket, 1848

About the Author

James F. Shea, B.A., M.A., CHT. is a Therapist, Counselor and Consultant, in business and private practice in Vancouver, B.C. He serves, at present, as the Director of the Quantum Empowerment Institute, where he offers both individual and group programs in the area of Transpersonal Empowerment. His lectures, workshops and seminars have proven powerfully inspirational and transformative, and James has become acknowledged for his Vision and skills developed over more than four decades. His eclectic approach draws on a Bachelor's and Master's Degree in Psychology with more advanced research in the area of Psycho-Spiritual Awakening being carried out at Centers in London, England and in San Francisco, USA. James has also been certified as a Clinical Hypnotherapist by the American Board of Clinical Hypnotherapy. In addition to his counselling practice, and his involvement in the Institute, James was involved for almost two decades with the Provincial Government in the establishment and support of alternative residential learning environments for the developmentally challenged.

Printed in the United States
By Bookmasters